At Issue

Guns and Crime

Other Books in the At Issue Series:

At Issue

| Guns and Crime

Christine Watkins, Book Editor

GREENHAVEN PRESS
A part of Gale, Cengage Learning

GALE
CENGAGE Learning·

Detroit • New York • San Francisco • New Haven, Conn • Waterville, Maine • London

Elizabeth Des Chenes, *Managing Editor*

© 2012 Greenhaven Press, a part of Gale, Cengage Learning.

Gale and Greenhaven Press are registered trademarks used herein under license.

For more information, contact:
Greenhaven Press
27500 Drake Rd.
Farmington Hills, MI 48331-3535
Or you can visit our Internet site at gale.cengage.com

Articles in Greenhaven Press anthologies are often edited for length to meet page requirements. In addition, original titles of these works are changed to clearly present the main thesis and to explicitly indicate the author's opinion. Every effort is made to ensure that Greenhaven Press accurately reflects the original intent of the authors. Every effort has been made to trace the owners of copyrighted material.

Cover Image copyright Illustration Works.

LIBRARY OF CONGRESS CATALOGING-IN-PUBLICATION DATA

Guns and crime / Christine Watkins, editor.
    p. cm. -- (At issue)
Includes bibliographical references and index.
ISBN 978-0-7377-5574-9 (hardcover) -- ISBN 978-0-7377-5575-6 (pbk.)
1. Gun control--United States. 2. Firearms and crime--United States. I. Watkins, Christine, 1951- II. Title. III. Series.
    HV7436.G87738 2013
    364.2--dc23
                                                    2011042810

Printed in the United States of America
2 3 4 5 6 7 16 15 14 13 12

Contents

Introduction

NRA. When most Americans see or hear those letters, the National Rifle Association of America immediately comes to mind, eliciting passionate feelings along with it. The NRA is reviled by some and revered by others. The mere mention of the organization can turn friends into foes, conversations into shouting matches, and create rifts between family members. Some people even believe the NRA holds sway over life and death situations. What is it about an association of hunters, shooting sports enthusiasts, and gun collectors that provokes such heated controversy and splits one nation into two almost equal factions?

The NRA was established shortly after the American Civil War to improve the marksmanship of potential soldiers, and is today still considered to be the leader in firearms training and education. Following World War II, the NRA expanded its interests to include hunting and shooting sports, such as skeet; as a result, the NRA's popularity grew along with its membership, taking on approximately three hundred thousand members. For several more years and throughout the 1950s, the NRA steadily increased its membership while primarily focusing on "Firearms Safety Education," "Marksmanship Training," and "Shooting for Recreation," as stated on its 1958 headquarters building. During this time, the organization's political interests were relatively moderate and relied more on educating members about hunting and wildlife issues than lobbying Congress. In fact, the NRA supported the government's National Firearms Act of 1934—which taxed and regulated the sale of machine guns and banned silencers and sawed-off shotguns—as well as the Federal Firearms Act of 1938, which along with licensing gun and ammunition makers, barred known felons from legally buying guns. Even into the 1960s when gun crime was becoming rampant in the United States, the NRA supported regulations to keep firearms away from felons, the mentally unstable, and minors. It was only when the government established a separate Bureau of Alcohol, Tobacco, and Firearms (ATF) in 1972 and continued to further restrict gun ownership and increase gun regulations that the NRA became especially concerned about safeguarding its fundamental principle that gun ownership is a civil liberty protected by the Second Amendment of the U.S. Constitution.

Thus, to counter the anti-gun activists, the organization created a formal lobbying branch called the Institute for Legislative Action (ILA), which became, and still is, a very active and formidable political presence. Today, with over four million dues-paying members, the NRA claims to be America's longest-lived civil rights organization and champions politicians who oppose gun control laws. According to Richard Feldman in his book *Ricochet: Confessions of a Gun Lobbyist,* "The association is probably the single most politically active lobbying group in the country." Feldman further mentions that the acronym NRA has been known to stand for "Never Re-elected Again" aimed at those politicians who dare to take a stand against the organization.

While the NRA views "the right of the people to keep and bear arms" as sacrosanct, many other Americans hold that view at least partly responsible for the staggering level of gun violence in the United States. Experts estimate that gun crime kills or injures 100,000 Americans every year. Put another way, approximately 264 people are killed or injured by guns every single day in the United States. According to the Children's Defense Fund, there are over 280 million guns in civilian hands in the United States, and every year an estimated 4.5 million new firearms, including 2 million handguns, are sold. "What is it with America and guns?" asks Ed Pilkington in his 2011 *Guardian* article "US Gun Crime: Death for Sale." Pilkington also asks, "Why does the most advanced democracy, which prides itself on being a bastion of reason and civilization in a brutal and ugly world, put up with this carnage in its own back yard?"

Why indeed. Just about half the nation thinks gun control laws should be the response. According to a 2011 *Washington Post*-ABC News poll, 52 percent of the American people favor stricter gun control. They believe that enforcing "common sense" gun laws—such as a ban on assault weapons and high-capacity ammunition magazines, mandatory background checks every time a firearm is sold, and mandatory reporting of stolen guns—can successfully reduce gun violence and better protect the public. Shortly after Jared Lee Loughner shot nineteen people, including US Representative Gabrielle Giffords, near Tucson, Arizona, on January 8, 2011, the article "President Obama: We Must Seek Agreement on Gun Reforms" appeared in the *Arizona Daily Star*. The editor wrote, "I'm willing to bet that responsible, law-abiding gun owners agree that we should be able to keep an irresponsible, law-breaking few—dangerous criminals and fugitives, for example—from getting their hands on a gun in the first place."

The NRA does not disagree and understands the frustration Americans feel about mass shootings and gun crime; however, it does not agree that disarming law-abiding citizens is the solution. Instead, the NRA is resolute in its conviction that self-defense is a fundamental right and still stands behind its 1985 position that the "greatest single deterrent to crime is an armed citizenry."

And so it appears that the nation has reached a stalemate with no compromise in sight. Brian Doherty explains in his 2008 book *Gun Control on Trial*, "Threaded through the political fight over gun control is a cultural fight and a feeling of danger on both sides. . . . And both think that the other side is full of people who simply do not mean well and cannot be trusted." The authors in *At Issue: Guns and Crime* discuss this and other perspectives regarding this passionately debated topic.

1

Guns and Gun Crime Are Widespread in America

Paul Harris

Paul Harris is a US correspondent for the British newspapers The Guardian *and* The Observer.

Despite the fact that gun crime is rampant in the United States and anti-gun groups clamor for stronger gun control laws, the prevalence of guns continues to escalate, from the suburbs to inner cities, from pistols to assault rifles. Critics of America's gun culture often blame the accessibility of guns for the high level of violent crime. But the powerful National Rifle Association (NRA), with more than three million members and untold millions of dollars to fund political agendas, has managed to keep gun ownership firmly entrenched in American society.

Shirley Katz is not afraid to fight for her rights. Last week [October 2007] the schoolteacher, 44, went to court in her home town of Medford, Oregon, to protest at her working conditions. Specifically she is outraged she cannot carry a handgun into class. 'I know it is my right to carry that gun,' she said.

Katz was in court in the week that someone else took a gun to school in America. This time it was a pupil in Cleveland, Ohio. Asa Coon, 14, walked the corridors of his school, a gun in each hand, shooting two teachers and two students. Then he killed himself. Coon's attempted massacre made headlines. But a more bloody rampage, the murder of six young partygoers by Tyler Peterson, a policeman in Crandon, Wisconsin, got less attention, even in the *New York Times*—America's newspaper of record—which buried it deep inside the paper.

Guns, and the violence their possessors inflict, have never been more prevalent in America. Gun crime has risen steeply over the past three years. Despite the fact groups such as the National Rifle Association (NRA) consistently claim they are being victimised, there have probably never been so many guns or gun-owners in America—although no one can be sure, as no one keeps a reliable account. One federal study estimated there were 215 million guns, with about half of all US households owning one. Such a staggering number makes America's gun culture thoroughly mainstream.

An average of almost eight people aged under 19 are shot dead in America everyday. In 2005 there were more than 14,000 gun murders in the US—with 400 of the victims children. There are 16,000 suicides by firearm and 650 fatal accidents in an average year. Since the killing of John F. Kennedy in 1963, more Americans have died by American gunfire than perished on foreign battlefields in the whole of the 20th century.

Studies show that having a gun at home makes it six times more likely that an abused woman will be murdered. A gun in a US home is 22 times more likely to be used in an accidental shooting, a murder or a suicide than in self-defence against an attack. Yet despite those figures US gun culture is not retreating. It is growing. Take Katz's case in Oregon. She brought her cause to court under a state law that gives licensed gun-owners the right to bring a firearm to work: her school is her workplace. Such a debate would have been unthinkable a few decades ago. Now it is the battleground. 'Who would have thought a few years ago, we would even be having this conversation? But this won't stop here,' said Professor Brian Anse

Patrick of the University of Toledo in Ohio. Needless to say, last week the judge sided with Katz and she won the first round of her case.

It is a nation awash with guns, from the suburbs to the inner cities and from the Midwest's farms to Manhattan's mansions. Gun-owning groups have been so successful in their cause that it no longer even seems strange to many Americans that Katz should want to go into an English class armed. 'They have made what was once unthinkable thinkable,' said Patrick, a liberal academic. He should know. He owns a gun himself. Even the US critics of gun culture are armed.

To look at the photographs in Kyle Cassidy's book *Armed America* is to glimpse a surreal world. Or at least it seems that way to many non-Americans. Cassidy spent two years taking portrait shots of gun owners and their weapons across the US.

The result is a disturbing tableau of happy families, often with pets and toddlers, posing with pistols, assault rifles and the sort of heavy machine-guns usually associated with a war-zone. 'By the end I had seen so many guns and I knew so much about guns that it no longer seemed unusual,' Cassidy said. He keeps his in a gun safe in his home in Philadelphia. 'This turned into a project not about guns but about a diverse group of people,' he said.

At the cutting edge of weapon culture remains the gun lobby and its most vocal advocate, the NRA. Founded in the 19th century by ex-Civil War army officers dismayed at their troops' lack of marksmanship, the NRA has transformed into the most effective lobbying group in Washington DC. It has scores of lobbyists, millions of dollars in funds and more than three million members. It is highly organised and its huge membership is highly motivated and activist. They can have a huge influence on politics.

In 2000 Vice-President Al Gore supported stricter background checks for gun-buyers and the NRA organised against him, describing the election as the most important since the

Civil War. It spent $20m against Gore in an election ending in a razor's edge result. Its influence was especially felt in Gore's home state of Tennessee, which he narrowly lost to NRA gloating. 'Their vote can select the President. They don't get to pick who goes to the White House. But they can tip the balance,' said Patrick.

The role of the gun is now enshrined in mass popular culture and has huge patriotic significance.

Democrats have learnt that lesson now. Many shy away from gun control issues, wary of taking on such a vociferous lobby group. In the 2006 mid-term elections the NRA was able to back a historically high 58 Democrats running for office. Every one of them went on to win. Such influence over the past three decades has seen the NRA fight a successful campaign against new gun laws. It has in fact loosened regulations, spreading the ability to legally carry concealed weapons across 39 states. And this has all been done in the face of a fight from anti-gun groups, backed by much of the mainstream media. 'Politicians are so afraid of the gun lobby. They run scared of it,' said Joan Burbick, author of the book *Gun Show Nation*.

But the key question is not about the number of guns in America; it is about why people are armed. For many gun-owners, and a few sociologists, the reason lies in America's past. The frontier society, they say, was populated by gun-wielding settlers who used weapons to feed their families and ward off hostile bandits and Indians. America was thus born with a gun in its hand. Unfortunately much of this history is simply myth. The vast majority of settlers were farmers, not fighters. The task of killing Indians was left to the military and—most effectively—European diseases. Guns in colonial times were much rarer than often thought, not least because they were so expensive that few settlers could afford them. Indeed one study of early gun homicides showed that a musket was as likely to be used as club to beat someone to death as actually fired.

But many Americans believe the myth. The role of the gun is now enshrined in mass popular culture and has huge patriotic significance. Hence the fact that gun ownership is still a constitutional right, in case America is ever invaded and needs to form a popular militia (as hard as that event might be to imagine). It also explains why guns are so prevalent in Hollywood. Currently playing in US cinemas is the Jodie Foster film *The Brave One*, a classic vigilante movie of the wronged woman turning to the power of the pistol to murder the criminals who killed her boyfriend. Foster's character is played as undeniably heroic. 'There is a fascination with guns in our culture. All you need to make a movie is a girl and a gun,' said Cassidy.

But this worship of the gun in many ways springs from economics and social problems, not the historic frontier. It took mass production and mass marketing to really popularise firearms. The Civil War saw mass arms manufacturing explode in America, including making 200,000 Colt .44 pistols alone. It saw guns become familiar and cheaper for millions of Americans. The later 19th century saw gun companies using marketing techniques to sell their weapons, often invoking invented frontier imagery to do so. That carries on today. There are more than 2,000 gun shows each year, selling hundreds of thousands of guns. It is big business and business needs to sell more and more guns to keep itself profitable. 'They will do anything to sell guns,' said Burbick.

But there are deeper issues at work too. The gun lobby's main argument is that guns protect their owners. They deter criminals and attackers whom—the gun lobby points out helpfully—are often armed themselves. Some surveys estimate there are more than two million 'defensive' uses of firearms each year. But others say that this argument is a shield, using guns as a way of deflecting harder arguments about how crime is caused by economics, poverty and racism. 'The argument over guns redefines a lot of social issues as simple aspects of crime,' said Burbick. She argues that a way to make Americans feel safer from crime is not to arm them with guns but to tackle the causes of crime: urban poverty, joblessness, drug addiction and racial divisions. 'We have to take back the language of human security. To talk about solving those social issues in terms of safety, not just letting the gun lobby control that language,' she said.

> The gun culture is so firmly entrenched and society so full of guns that there is little prospect of it retreating.

It is a powerful argument. Critics of America's gun culture often point to other nations with high levels of gun ownership—such as Canada and Switzerland—but much lower levels of violent crime. The fact is that America itself is equally divided. Patrick lives in a quiet, rural part of Michigan just across the state line from Ohio and the town of Toledo where he works. 'I would be amazed if anyone within four miles of me did not have a gun,' he said 'But our homicide rate is zero.'

Then look at where Cassidy lives. He has an apartment in Philadelphia, a city that is just as flooded with guns as Patrick's rural idyll, but also suffers from inner-city social ills. It has a stratospheric murder rate. 'There is a murder here every day. This is something that America has to come to terms with,' he said. Yet the differences do not lie with the simple existence of guns. Both places are full of them. They lie with the root causes of crime and violence, such as poverty and drugs, that blight many big cities. Guns seem neither to be totally the problem and certainly not the solution.

However, that is a debate few in America are having. In the meantime, the gun culture is so firmly entrenched and society so full of guns that there is little prospect of it retreating.

Even those who advocate much tighter laws have long accepted defeat of the ideal of creating a society where guns are rare in public life, or even completely absent. 'That notion is absurd. There is no way to de-gun America,' said Patrick.

To cap a grim week, as Katz was winning her court battle in Oregon police in Pennsylvania were giving details of a raid on the home of a teenager who was plotting to attack a school. They found seven home-made grenades and an assault rifle. His mother had bought it for him at a gun show. The boy was just 14.

2

The Accessibility of Guns Leads to Gun Crime

Alan M. Ruben

Alan M. Ruben is a physician in Wheeling, West Virginia.

The question often arises: Would Americans be safer if more people owned guns? The answer is a definite No. More guns just means more gun crime and deaths. After all, firearm injuries are the second leading cause of injury death in the United States, and the rate of gun-related deaths among US children under the age of fifteen is nearly twelve times higher than that among children in twenty-five other industrialized nations combined. Furthermore, there is no credible evidence that permitting citizens to carry concealed firearms reduces crime. There is, however, evidence that permissive concealed carry laws may actually increase crime. It should be obvious that easy access to deadly weapons is responsible for the deaths of too many Americans.

Let's be honest about the purpose of a firearm. It is not a decoration for the wall of your den or a trinket to display for your friends. It is a device created for the sole purpose of killing a person or an animal. Let's put aside the matter of whether you own a rifle for use in hunting animals. What remains are handguns. Handguns are designed specifically to kill people with maximum efficiency. So here's the critical question Americans need to ask: Are we, our loved ones and our community safer if we and our neighbors own handguns? Let's try to answer that question in a FAQ [frequently asked questions] format.

How common are deaths and injuries from handguns in America?

Firearm injuries are the second leading cause of injury death in the U.S., and have killed more than 28,000 Americans each year since 1972.

In a single year, 2007, guns took the lives of 31,224 Americans in homicides, suicides and accidental shootings. This is more than 85 gun-related deaths a day—three deaths every hour of every day. Furthermore, about 70,000 Americans were treated in hospital emergency rooms for non-fatal gunshot wounds in 2007. Guns were the third leading cause of injury related deaths nationwide in 2007 following motor vehicle accidents and poisoning.

In the first seven years of the Iraq War, 4,400 soldiers were killed. Almost as many civilians are killed with guns in the U.S. every month.

Well, don't other countries have a problem similar to ours?

The United States has by far the highest rate of gun deaths—murders, suicides and accidents—among the world's 36 richest nations.

U.S. homicide rates are 6.9 times higher than rates in 22 other populous high-income countries combined, despite similar non-lethal crime and violence rates. The firearm homicide rate in the U.S. is 19.5 times higher.

The overall firearm-related death rate among U.S. children under the age of 15 is nearly 12 times higher than that among children in 25 other industrialized nations combined.

All right, I understand that there is a human cost to gun violence, but is there also an economic cost that affects me as a taxpayer?

Firearm-related deaths and injuries result in estimated medical costs of $2.3 billion each year—half of which are borne by U.S. taxpayers.

Once all the direct and indirect medical, legal and societal costs are factored together, the annual cost of gun violence in America amounts to $100 billion.

I have heard that if the majority of people own guns, criminals would be frightened and crimes would be prevented. So, if there are more gun owners in my state than in surrounding states, members of my family should be safer. Is this true?

Regions and states with higher rates of gun ownership have significantly greater rates of homicide than states with lower rates of gun ownership.

Gun death rates are seven times higher in the states with the highest gun ownership compared with states with the lowest household gun ownership.

States with the highest levels of gun ownership have 114 percent higher firearm murder rates and 60 percent higher total homicide rates than states with the lowest gun ownership.

My sister is divorcing her husband and they are fighting over custody of the kids. Her husband owns a handgun. Is she in greater danger from domestic violence because of the gun?

Abused women are five times more likely to be killed by their abuser if the abuser owns a firearm.

Regions and states with higher rates of gun ownership have significantly greater rates of homicide.

Firearms were used to kill more than two-thirds of spouse and ex-spouse homicide victims between 1990 and 2005.

I worry about my kids, too. Are they in greater danger because we have a gun in our house? Their friends' parents also own guns. Should I worry about that, too?

Guns cause the death of 20 children and young adults (24 years of age and under) each day in the U.S. Children and young adults (24 years of age and under) suffer over 41 percent of all firearm deaths and non-fatal injuries.

From 2001 through 2007, over 4,900 people in the United States died from unintentional shootings. Over 1,750 victims of unintentional shootings between 2001 and 2007 were under 25 years of age.

The firearm-related suicide rate for children between the ages of 5 and 14 years old in the United States is nearly 11 times higher than that in 25 other developed countries.

A U.S. Secret Service study of 37 school shootings in 26 states found that in nearly two-thirds of the incidents, the attacker got the gun from his or her own home or that of a relative.

But people say having a gun in our house is necessary for protection. If someone breaks into our house, shouldn't we have a gun to defend ourselves? And, if we shoot someone like that, isn't it a "justifiable homicide" rather than a crime? Surely having a gun in our house makes us safer?

A gun kept in the home is 22 times more likely to be used in an unintentional shooting, a criminal assault or homicide, or an attempted or completed suicide than to be used to injure or kill in self defense. Rather than conferring protection, guns in the home are associated with three times the risk of homicide by a family member or intimate acquaintance.

There is no credible statistical evidence that permissive concealed carry laws reduce crime.

There were 13,636 Americans who were murdered in 2009. Of this, only 215 were killed by firearms in shootings by private citizens that law enforcement determined were justifiable homicide.

From 2001 through 2007, over 4,900 people in the United States died from unintentional shootings. Over 1,750 victims of unintentional shootings between 2001 and 2007 were under 25 years of age.

Congresswoman Gabrielle Giffords [was shot] and a federal judge [was] murdered in Tucson, Ariz., [January 2011] by an armed psychopath. Wouldn't it have been better if bystanders had concealed weapons to kill him before he was able to fire so many bullets?

Permitting the carrying of concealed firearms does not appear to reduce crimes. There is no credible statistical evidence that permissive concealed carry laws reduce crime. There is evidence that permissive concealed carry laws generally will increase crime.

Isn't it true that gun dealers must do background checks to prevent selling guns to known criminals and people with psychiatric illnesses?

The Bureau of Alcohol, Tobacco and Firearms reviewed over 1,500 of its investigations and concluded that gun shows are a "major trafficking channel," associated with approximately 26,000 firearms diverted from legal to illegal commerce. Gun shows rank second to corrupt dealers as a source for illegally trafficked firearms.

It is estimated that over 40 percent of gun acquisitions occur in the secondary market. That means that they happen without any background check whatsoever.

There is reason to feel optimistic that good sense may prevail, and Americans will finally recover from their long, unwholesome romance with guns. The NRA [National Rifle Association] promoted notion that "packing heat" is as American as apple pie is coming under attack. Experts are questioning the wisdom of easy access to deadly weapons that has caused the death and misery of so many Americans. It is becoming obvious that we need the same restrictions on gun ownership as exist in almost every other civilized country.

Let's conclude with a story that you might very well read in the *Wheeling News-Register*, Feb. 24, 2015: The NRA has lobbied mightily and has finally convinced the West Virginia State Legislature to pass an unrestricted concealed carry law; most citizens now carry their pistols every day for self-defense.

It is the final round of the Big East Basketball tournament in Morgantown pitting WVU [West Virginia University] against its closest rival, Pittsburgh. In the stands, a drunken student, enraged by a taunt he has heard, draws his weapon and fires several shots. Hundreds in the stands duck for cover while reaching for their loaded weapons. Dozens rise up and start firing at the person they believe to be the shooter. A few guess right and bring him down. Many others guess wrong, and shoot instead the first person they see with gun in hand. In the ensuing crossfire, several students die and many others are injured.

3

The Accessibility of Guns
Protects Lives

David M. Huntwork

David M. Huntwork is a conservative activist, blogger, and columnist, and is the site administrator for the Constitution Club blog.

Empowering people to protect themselves and others against criminals makes perfect sense, and the more law-abiding citizens carrying guns, the safer Americans will be. Anti-gun advocates often exaggerate the risks of mass shoot-outs or accidental killings. But, in fact, concealed-carry permit holders have better safety records than police officers, and more criminals are killed by citizens defending themselves than are killed by law enforcement.

I am a concealed handgun permit holder in the state of Colorado. I can, and often do, carry a firearm in McDonalds, Wal-Mart, the mall, and most anywhere else the average citizen goes. A small circle of public safety if you will, not just for my family and me but for those fellow citizens that cross my path throughout the day. Yet I, or any other law-abiding citizen, cannot carry on school campuses.

The Concealed Handgun Permit

I initially applied for my concealed handgun permit a month or so before 9-11. The fee was $100 payable to the county and a $35 CBI [Colorado Bureau of Investigation] background fee.

As soon as 9-11 occurred the local sheriff waived the $100 county fee and proceeded to hand out concealed carry permits as quickly as possible. Mine was permit number 1768 and within just a couple months the local sheriff issued about 5,000 more. In the years since then I am not aware of a single permit holder who has been involved in any firearm-related crime. Those who argue against concealed carry permit laws or forbid them in certain areas are, at best, incredibly ignorant and at worst purposelessly exposing their fellow countrymen to violent crime, assaults, and even death for the sake of ideology and feel good politics.

The truth is often very simple. The law-abiding, gun-owning citizen is not the problem but for some reason is often the target of those who seek to disarm the populace.

Every argument I have seen opposing the right to conceal carry is mere hysteria about guns in general and not rooted in reality.

When I received my concealed handgun permit it required little more than having the right sheriff, taking a hunters safety course, filling out a questionnaire, not having a criminal record, and writing a check. They have since tightened the restrictions a bit, but not by much if you know the right [National Rifle Association] NRA instructor. Seventy-five dollars can get you an afternoon of target practice, training, and your ticket to the coveted concealed-carry permit if you are willing to do your homework.

Think of the growing number of concealed handgun permit holders as thousands of walking safety bubbles moving throughout society and undoubtedly crossing your path while potentially protecting you and your family without you even knowing it. You can live as a victim subject to the whim of criminals and crazies or you can live as a free man and have the potential to protect yourself, your family, and your community. I choose the latter.

Common Sense over Misinformation

Advocating that law-abiding citizens have the right to protect themselves from massacre, rape, assault, and robbery is hardly being partisan. In fact, it is because conservatives care about their fellow citizens that they hate to see the failed, hand-wringing policies that provide "criminal safe" zones where such people can act with impunity.

Every argument I have seen opposing the right to conceal carry is mere hysteria about guns in general and not rooted in reality. There are some times when you may not be sure whether you are on the correct side of an issue, but on this there is no doubt. Few things could be clearer to those who seek to be guided by logic and common sense.

Doesn't it just make you sick watching people die and the law not allowing a single one of them to be prepared to defend themselves? Concealed-carry permit holders have better safety records than police forces themselves, and fewer cases statistically of misusing their firearms. So the argument that "guns in the hands of private citizens are bad no matter what the circumstances" is incredibly ignorant, sad, and misinformed. And such sentiments create the climate that prevents such incredible tragedies from themselves being limited and stopped once they begin. I get angry and upset when I see such things. I believe in empowering people, not treating them like children.

The ability of a man to bear arms, whether his antagonist be foreign or domestic, a rogue government or a savage criminal, is a fundamental right of being a free man. That right is no less important, and many would argue even more so, than the right to free speech, assembly, press, or the freedom to worship God without government supervision, permission, or persecution. A man has not just the right, but the inherent obligation to protect his children, family, neighbors, community, and nation. One has to ask the question why it is so threatening to some for a few people to be allowed to carry concealed handguns in society. Is the thought of responsible citizens being allowed to protect themselves and others in the unlikely event of armed violence in their immediate vicinity really that terrorizing? What are they afraid of other than factual contradictions to their stated ideology that all guns are always bad in all situations? The real world tells us a different story.

Utopian ideals and unworkable solutions will not solve or prevent tragic incidents at schools, churches, and malls. It is incredible that in a post 9-11 world the citizens of this nation are forced to be helpless and vulnerable by both the law and institutional policies by people who cannot provide even the most elementary security to those it has disarmed.

People are alive today because a fellow citizen was able to use a firearm to save their lives.

The only school shootings that have ever been stopped were by armed citizens/teachers who had relatively quick access to a firearm (in several instances they had one stashed in a vehicle in the parking lot) and were able to take the necessary measures to save lives. Yet that is what many have deemed to be unacceptable.

Why would you disarm law-abiding citizens in an attempt to stop criminals who neither respect the law nor abide by it? Logic and common sense should dictate our solutions and guide our hands, not misguided policies dictated solely by ideological nuances instead of simple facts.

The Right to Protect Yourself

Most people who have concealed-carry permits are either ex-military or ex-law enforcement (I am neither for the record). The rest tend to be firearm enthusiasts who either have grown up using firearms since they were children or have had extensive experience with them. I cannot find a single case where a law-abiding citizen with a handgun intervening to stop a public/school shooting ended up with several additional people shot than there otherwise would have been. That simply doesn't happen. But there are multiple examples of attempted mass shootings where guns in the hands of law abiding citizens either thwarted the attempted massacre or brought an early end to the rampage.

We've seen multiple examples of the armed citizen scenario in play, and the results are encouraging. People are alive today because a fellow citizen was able to use a firearm to save their lives. This is not a Right/Left issue, nor should it be. It is an issue of protecting lives, empowering our citizens, and making our society and our current "gun free" zones far safer than they are today. I simply believe that people should have the choice to protect themselves and to be empowered against the criminal element and walking time bombs that prey upon the rest of society. What better issue to agree on than this one?

Despite the declaration of "gun free" zones, nearly thirty percent of all school shootings ever attempted have been thwarted by a law-abiding citizen with a firearm. No amount of explanation or analysis will ever take away the pain of the families, and no law or policy may have necessarily stopped any particular tragedy. All we can do is strive to empower people so that they can be protected and exercise their right to self-defense, while at the same time doing all that we can as a society to locate and prevent the "walking time bombs" among us from going off.

Courage should be honored while self-reliance, self-respect, good citizenship, patriotism, and personal responsibility should be taught and promoted. Instead it is mocked and subjugated while we are continually spoon-fed the poisoned gruel that we must rely on government for everything, including our own self-protection. Government can be good but over-reliance on it is deadly to a culture, and can be to the individual as well.

Guns are used some two million times a year to stop violent crimes in the general population. More criminals are killed by citizens defending themselves than by law enforcement. Some of this would undoubtedly transfer over to "criminal safe havens" such as college campuses if the utopian anti-gun laws were changed.

No one should insist on leaving entire sections of the community open and helpless to the predations of murderous psychopaths. It is important to attempt to help change a culture that has wandered hopelessly off the path of logic and common sense, and help to rectify the pathetically failed policies that cost some people their lives. I can think of nothing more important to address than that. People are dead because of others' stupidity and continual striving for a utopian nanny state. That cannot be excused or allowed to continue anymore.

Free Americans should have the right to defend themselves from the more unsavory elements of society that attempt to prey upon or outright kill them.

> *Laws that forbid the carrying of arms . . . disarm only those who are neither inclined nor determined to commit crimes . . . Such laws make things worse for the assaulted and better for the assailants; they serve rather to encourage than to prevent homicides, for an unarmed man may be attacked with greater confidence than an armed man.*
>
> *—[Thomas] Jefferson's "Commonplace Book," 1774–1776, quoting from* On Crimes and Punishment, *by criminologist Cesare Beccaria, 1764.*

4

Stronger Gun Control Laws Will Save Lives

Legal Community Against Violence

The Legal Community Against Violence (LCAV) is a national public interest law center dedicated to preventing gun violence and to providing legal assistance in support of gun violence prevention.

With nearly 400,000 gun crimes committed every year, the United States has the highest rate of firearm deaths (more than 30,000 each year) among twenty-five high-income nations. Clearly, stronger and more effective gun control laws are needed to keep guns out of the wrong hands and to better protect the public. Furthermore, despite what the gun lobby claims, most Americans are in favor of common-sense gun laws because they understand that such laws will, in fact, help reduce gun violence.

If guns really kept us safe, the United States would be the safest nation in the world, since we own an estimated 270 million firearms—approximately 90 guns for every 100 people. Far from keeping us safe, guns are used to kill more than 30,000 Americans each year and injure approximately 70,000. Guns are also used to commit nearly 400,000 crimes each year. The rate of firearm violence in America far exceeds that of other industrialized nations, where gun ownership is strictly regulated.

Although many people own guns for self-protection, studies have repeatedly shown that a gun in the home increases the risk of firearm-related death or injury to a household member. According to those studies, a gun kept in the home is more likely to be involved in an accidental shooting, criminal assault or suicide attempt than to be used to injure or kill an intruder in self-defense.

Convicted felons and other prohibited persons are able to buy guns easily from unlicensed sellers in undocumented transactions.

In addition, no evidence exists to support the claim that society would be safer if more people carried concealed guns in public. Evidence shows that permissive concealed carry laws may increase crime. Moreover, common sense tells us that putting more guns into more hands does not make anyone safer: it merely increases the odds that everyday disputes will escalate into deadly encounters.

The fact is that very few federal laws regulate the manufacture, sale or possession of firearms, and those currently on the books are filled with loopholes or significantly tie the hands of law enforcement. The Brady Act, for example, which requires licensed firearms dealers to perform background checks on gun purchasers, does not apply to private sellers, responsible for an estimated 40 percent of all gun sales. Because of this "private sale" loophole, convicted felons and other prohibited persons are able to buy guns easily from unlicensed sellers in undocumented transactions.

Even when a gun is purchased through a firearms dealer, another loophole permits the dealer to transfer the gun to the purchaser if the background check isn't completed within three days. These "default proceeds" allowed nearly 4,000 prohibited persons to purchase guns between November 1998 and November 1999 alone. In addition:

- Federal law doesn't ban military-style assault weapons, 50 caliber rifles or large capacity ammunition magazines. Congress allowed the 1994 ban on assault weapons and large capacity magazines to expire in 2004, despite overwhelming public support for the law. As a result, assault weapons, 50 caliber rifles and large capacity magazines have proliferated on the civilian market.

• Because federal law exempts guns from the Consumer Product Safety Act, no federal health and safety standards exist for domestically manufactured firearms, though such standards do exist for all other consumer products manufactured in America.

Given the loopholes and unreasonable restrictions in our nation's gun laws, it makes no sense to argue that we should merely "enforce the laws we already have." We need to strengthen existing laws to give law enforcement the tools they need to keep guns out of the wrong hands, and to ensure that firearms do not endanger public safety.

The sad reality is that gun violence affects all segments of our society. As newspaper headlines regularly show, deadly shootings occur in areas which are supposed to be the safest—including schools, places of worship, office buildings, shopping centers and nursing homes. In addition, unintentional shootings and suicides, while less publicized, occur every day nationwide. No one is immune from the devastation caused by the easy access to guns.

Although the U.S. Supreme Court held, in *District of Columbia v. Heller*, 128 S. Ct. 2783 (2008), that the Second Amendment protects the right to possess a firearm in the home for self-defense, the Court made clear that the Second Amendment permits a wide variety of strong gun laws. The Court provided examples of laws it considered "presumptively valid," including those which:

• Prohibit firearm possession by felons and the mentally ill;

- Forbid firearm possession in sensitive places such as schools and government buildings; and

- Impose conditions on the commercial sale of firearms.

The Court noted that this list is not exhaustive, and concluded that the Second Amendment is also consistent with laws banning "dangerous and unusual weapons" not in common use at the time, such as M-16 rifles and other firearms for military service. In addition, the Court declared that its analysis should not be read to suggest "the invalidity of laws regulating the storage of firearms to prevent accidents."

Finally, because the Heller case involved a law enacted by Washington, D.C., a federal enclave, the Court did not address the issue of whether the Second Amendment applies to state and local governments.

Sensible gun laws can and do work. Since the Brady Act went into effect in 1994, for example, background checks on prospective gun purchasers have prevented the sale of firearms to more than 1.6 million prohibited purchasers, notwithstanding that law's "private sale" loophole. In addition, studies have shown that a variety of state laws have had a positive impact and can serve as "best practices" for other states:

- Virginia's one-gun-a-month law, enacted to address gun trafficking, significantly reduced the number of out of state crime guns traced back to Virginia dealers.

- In 12 states where child access prevention laws had been in effect for at least one year, unintentional firearm deaths fell by 23% from 1990–94 among children under age 15.

- Following Maryland's adoption of a ban on "junk guns," firearm homicides dropped by 8.6% in the state—an average of 40 lives saved per year—between 1990 and 1998.

Two recent studies looked at the impact of gun laws more broadly. The first report, released by Mayors Against Illegal Guns (MAIG) in 2008, focused on the relationship between a state's gun laws and the likelihood the state would be a source of guns recovered in out-of-state crimes.

The MAIG report found that states with the highest crime gun export rates—i.e., states that were the top sources of guns recovered in crime across state lines—had the weakest gun laws. That report also found that states that export crime guns at a high rate have a significantly higher rate of gun murders than states with low export rates; and a significantly higher rate of fatal police shootings than states with low export rates.

The second study, released by The Violence Policy Center in 2009, found that states with weak gun laws and high rates of gun ownership have the highest rates of gun death. Conversely, the study found that states with strong gun laws and low rates of gun ownership had significantly lower rates of firearm-related death.

U.S. gun laws are among the most lax in the world.

Sensible gun laws do not "punish" law abiding citizens—they save lives. Legislators nationwide have enacted laws to protect public safety, despite the fact they may impose a small burden on law-abiding citizens and despite the fact that some people will ignore them. For example, we have laws regulating automobiles and automobile drivers (such as speed limits and the use of seat belts), even though some people may find those laws inconvenient and others will violate them. Similarly, laws regulating guns and gun owners (such as requiring buyers to undergo a background check or banning the sale of assault weapons) protect the public, despite the fact that some may find them burdensome and others may ignore them. The reality is that most Americans support sensible gun laws because they realize those laws help reduce gun violence.

Although our society has become desensitized to high levels of gun deaths and injuries, gun violence is not normal and should not be accepted as an unavoidable part of life in an industrialized country. Gun violence is, in fact, relatively rare in other industrialized nations. Studies have shown that:

- The U.S. has the highest rate of firearm deaths among 25 high-income nations.

- The overall firearm-related death rate among U.S. children under the age of 15 is nearly 12 times higher than that among children in 25 other industrialized nations combined.

The reasons for this great disparity are clear: Americans own far more civilian firearms—particularly handguns—than people in other industrialized nations, and U.S. gun laws are among the most lax in the world.

Although some opponents of strong gun laws—particularly those requiring gun owners to register their firearms or obtain a license—claim these laws will lead to governmental confiscation, there is simply no evidence to support this claim. If it were true, confiscation of lawfully-owned guns would have taken place in jurisdictions that already require gun owners to register their guns or obtain a license (e.g. Hawaii, New York, New Jersey, California, Massachusetts, Illinois, Cleveland and Omaha). The gun lobby can point to no such evidence, however. Moreover, the "slippery slope/confiscation" argument has been taken off the table by the Supreme Court's interpretation of the Second Amendment.

Although many elected officials are reluctant to support rational gun laws because they fear voter rejection, that fear is unfounded. A report by the Brady Campaign to Prevent Gun Violence following the 2008 elections found "no evidence that any candidate, at any level, lost because of support for sensible gun laws. Supporters of common sense gun laws won in Senate, House and state races across the country."

These findings are consistent with nationwide polling data, which show overwhelming public support for rational gun laws. Those polls show, for example, that:

- 92% of respondents, including 91% of gun owners, favor mandatory criminal background checks for all gun purchasers.

- 83% of respondents, including 72% of gun owners, favor registration for newly-purchased handguns, and 85% of respondents, including 73% of gun owners, favor laws requiring handgun purchasers to obtain a permit.

- 65% of respondents favor banning military style assault weapons, and 74.9% favor governmental safety standards for firearms.

This is the grand-daddy of all gun myths. It is used by opponents of sensible gun laws to convey the idea that it is somehow unfair to regulate guns, since human intervention is generally required to fire a gun. That fact, while generally true, does not lead to the conclusion that guns should be free from governmental regulation. Indeed, our laws regulate the sale and possession of other dangerous instrumentalities, such as automobiles, despite the fact that one could also say that "cars don't kill people, people kill people." Automobiles, unlike guns, are subject to a myriad of federal health and safety standards to protect their owners and the public.

To the extent it is accurate to say that "people kill people" with guns, the gun lobby should actually be supportive of laws that require gun buyers and owners to demonstrate they are able to possess firearms lawfully and responsibly, such as those requiring purchasers to pass a background check, obtain a license and register their firearms.

5

Gun Control Laws Will Not Save Lives

Stephen E. Wright

Stephen E. Wright writes the blog "From the Bluff" and is the author of the book Off Road: A Uniquely American Novel About God, Guns, Big Trucks . . . and Family.

When trying to solve the serious problem of violence in America, anti-gun groups continually focus on gun ownership and reiterate old arguments that studies have proven to be false. For example, gun control advocates claim that if individuals are allowed to carry concealed firearms, more gun fights will occur. The fact is, however, that law-abiding citizens are already permitted to carry concealed guns in forty states, and no increase in shoot-outs has resulted. Furthermore, thousands of citizens have been able to save their own lives with firearms because a gun was available to them.

So when faced with the most complex and serious issue in America, our culture of violence, why do anti-gun groups continue to restate old arguments that have been disproven so many times? Why do they continue to expend their efforts to fight battles that restrict a constitutional right but do nothing to make our society safer? Is it not also common sense that it is what is in the heart, not the hand, of a person that makes them a murderer? . . .

Here are oft heard anti-gun group "common sense gun laws" supported by nothing but emotional rhetoric and still promoted no matter how many times they're disproven.

Handgun Purchases Should Not Be Limited

Emotional Rhetoric: One Handgun per month—a law limiting people to a single handgun purchase per month will reduce trafficking in guns to criminals. The theory is that handguns are frequently purchased legally in bulk and resold on the "black market."

Fact: While there have been prosecuted cases of people buying multiple handguns and reselling them to criminals, the ATF [Bureau of Alcohol, Tobacco, Firearms and Explosives] already requires a report from an FFL [federal firearms license] of anyone who buys two or more handguns within a 6-day period. Which means multiple purchases by gun smugglers are rare and are, or should be, always investigated. Most handguns used in crimes are stolen and passed frequently from criminal to criminal or purchased not by mass gun buyers but by a friend or relation—which would not be affected by "one handgun a month."

Real Common Sense: The impact of a one handgun a month law would affect only a tiny percentage of the illegal gun market. And in the illegal gun market, like all unregulated markets (i.e. drugs), money will always find a supply. If one of the numerous sources of guns to criminals dries up others will take up the slack. And while it's true that 1 gun per month/12 guns per year would satisfy most shooters, why write a new law and create more bureaucracy unless it actually helps? If it won't save any lives but restricts honest gun collectors, is it a good law?

Large Capacity Magazines Should Not Be Banned

Emotional Rhetoric: Large capacity firearms magazines enable murderers to kill large numbers of victims. The basic argument that having 15 bullets in a single magazine instead of 10 makes a gun more lethal.

Fact: During the [April 1999] Columbine massacre (where many victims were killed with a normal pump shotgun) [Eric] Harris had only 10-round magazines for his 9mm, as did [Seung-Hui] Cho at the Virginia Tech massacre [April 2007] for one of his pistols. It takes 2 seconds or less to change the magazine in a weapon, which is simply not an impediment for an armed man shooting unarmed victims. And in any case most criminal activities, including the murders of police officers, involve very few shots fired (on average 3–4). The number of rounds a magazine can hold is simply not important and does not affect the lethality of a weapon.

Real Common Sense: Which is most frightening: A deranged killer intent on mass murder walking into your child's school with a pistol with 10-round magazines, a pistol with 15-round magazines, a pump shotgun, or a revolver? The fact is all are equally frightening visualizations. It does not take a specific type of weapon or a certain number of rounds to commit a mass murder; it takes a madman and a contained group of victims with no ability to defend themselves. Charles Whitman, for decades the mass murderer shooter with the greatest body count, had NO weapons capable of holding more than 10 rounds. And in any case, the deadliest mass murders do not involve firearms at all. Twist statistics any way you want, but it is what is in the heart of a mass murderer, not what is in their hand, that determines their lethality. Or in the simplest terms, where there is madness there is a way.

It is what is in the heart of a mass murderer, not what is in their hand, that determines their lethality

---

Concealed Guns Should Be Allowed

Emotional Rhetoric: Concealed carry of guns by normal citizens will end up with blood in the streets! The OK corral! People having gun fights over parking spaces! It will be the

Wild West all over again! Basically, "normal" people can't be trusted with weapons to defend themselves or their families, and it is best if they endure whatever assault is made against them until real police arrive to fill out a report and issue a warrant for the attackers.

Fact: "Shall Issue" concealed carry laws, which allow ANY law abiding citizen to carry a concealed pistol, have spread to 40 states across the US since 1987. Millions of "average" Americans exercise this right, and there have been no explosions of crime, shootouts over parking spots, or road rage gunfights.

There are numerous verifiable cases of civilians using firearms for effective self-defense every day.

Real Common Sense: A normal citizen doesn't suddenly become a murderer because s/he has access to a firearm. There is a gigantic leap between the emotions that cause a person to make an obscene gesture, shout angry words, or even throw a punch and the murderous rage that makes someone draw a handgun and kill a fellow human in other than self defense—an act which not only ends a life but also puts the shooter in jail. Average citizens don't go to this level no matter how mad they get, and those so deranged are already carrying weapons and already dangerous (which is all the more reason the rest of us need this option).

Guns Are Not Used Against the Owner

Emotional Rhetoric: People who try to protect their homes with guns will have them taken away and get shot with their own gun.

Fact: This never happens. There are numerous verifiable cases of civilians using firearms for effective self-defense every day, and virtually none of burglars taking away guns and shooting the homeowner or his family. Just try to find one.

Real Common Sense: A burglar intending to steal a stereo doesn't find a gun and decide to commit murder. If confronted by a homeowner, particularly an armed homeowner, he is most likely going to flee to find an easier mark. If he is breaking in to commit a violent act he already has sufficient weapons to do what he intends, which is all the more reason the homeowner needs to be empowered to fight back.

More Guns Do Not Result in More Accidental Shootings

Emotional Rhetoric: More guns means more gun accidents.

Fact: While it is true that if there were NO guns there would be NO gun accidents, a magically gun-free nation is impossible to achieve. But it is a fact that fatal gun accidents have reduced in number much faster than gun ownership has increased. And in every household there are dangerous items— household cleaners, swimming pools, and other items that cause many more accidental deaths than guns. . . .

Real Common Sense: Guns don't go off unless someone pulls the trigger. By properly handling a weapon there is no chance of an accidental discharge that will harm anyone. By keeping the gun properly secured there is no chance of a small child finding it and hurting himself or someone else.

Anti-Gun Groups Misconstrue the Facts

So why do anti-gun groups continue to define "common sense" in such a proven irrational manner and not put their resources into real solutions to America's culture of violence?

The emotional "common sense" belief of anti-gun groups is simple:

- America suffers from an outrageously disproportionate number of murders, mostly involving firearms, because of "lax" gun laws vs. countries with gun bans.

- The 2nd Amendment concept of civilian-owned firearms as a balance of power to a centralized government is outdated and no longer true.

- We are all safer if we take guns out of society—with perhaps the begrudging exception of very limited and highly tracked hunting rifles.

Fact: America does have a wildly disproportionate number of murders vs. other western countries.

- But two Western countries often used for comparison by anti-gun groups, Australia and the United Kingdom, had dramatically lower murder rates than the US before they instituted draconian anti-gun measures, and they still have lower rates afterwards.

- In fact, there was virtually NO effect on the overall murder rate in either nation, with homicide rates and even gun crime continuing to increase after their gun bans took effect. . . .

- Given that we know from experience that a large percentage of gun crimes continue in countries after total gun bans, and a percentage of murders transfer to non-gun murders after a gun ban, it would appear that a total gun ban in the US would have the same effect as elsewhere—none whatsoever on the overall murder rate.

America has a problem with violence culture, not a gun culture.

Real Common Sense:

- A person doesn't commit murder or a robbery because they have a weapon available, they choose to commit murder or a robbery and then find the means to do it.

- In the US depending on whom you want to believe tens of thousands or even millions of citizens defend their lives with firearms every year. . . .

- America has a problem with violence culture, not a gun culture. Guns are used by violent people too frequently in this country, but guns are not responsible for creating violent people, they created themselves. We have real issues in this country, but they are social issues and are reasons to promote, not restrict, civilian gun ownership until we find a social solution that works.

- Self defense and gun ownership are long and cherished traditions in the US, and surrendering them would NOT make us safer; quite the contrary, both as individuals and as a nation we would be much, much more endangered.

- For better or worse, America is a nation of individualists who are not afraid to fight back and take take charge of their own security (with the possible exception of a few large metropolitan populations on the east and west coasts). We need to deal with our problems of violence, but banning guns will weaken us and make our lives more dangerous, not less.

And as long as this post has been (is anyone really still reading—oh, I guess you are) how could I end it without my favorite quote from Benjamin Franklin, "They who can give up essential liberty to obtain a little temporary safety, deserve neither liberty nor safety."

6

The Background Check System Is Ineffective in Preventing Gun Violence

Colin Goddard

Colin Goddard is a survivor of the April 2007 shooting at Virginia Polytechnic Institute and State University in which gunman Seung-Hui Cho killed thirty-two people. Goddard has since become a gun control activist, is the assistant director for federal legislation at the Brady Center to Prevent Gun Violence, and filmed the 2010 documentary Living for 32.

Just about any adult can go to a gun show in the United States and buy a gun, whether it be a small pistol or an AK-47, without showing identification or passing a background check. As a result, Seung-Hui Cho, with a record of mental health problems, was able to open fire on classrooms at Virginia Polytechnic Institute and State University in April 2007, killing and wounding many students and teachers. To help prevent such disasters from happening again and to keep firearms from reaching the hands of people known to be dangerous, the background check system should be improved. Specifically, private sellers as well as licensed dealers must be obligated to perform background checks on every gun purchaser.

Now, the fact is Congressmen, I wouldn't be sitting in front of you today if it weren't for the events that took place at Virginia Tech [Virginia Polytechnic Institute and State

Colin Goddard, "Testimony before the Crime Sub-Committee of the U.S. House Judiciary Committee, July 14, 2010," Brady Campaign to Prevent Gun Violence (blog), July 15, 2010. http://blog.bradycampaign.org. Copyright © 2010 by Brady Campaign to Prevent Gun Violence. All rights reserved. Reproduced by permission.

University] on April 16th, 2007. I wouldn't be sitting in front of you today if it weren't for the 10 minutes of hell that I survived on that day.

And I wouldn't be sitting in front of you today if it weren't for all the things I have learned in my search for answering "Why" and "How" am I still alive.

In the Midst of the Shooting

What started off as a typical day in a small town school in southwest Virginia, soon further expanded our definition of the worst mass-shooting in US history. Midway through my 9:00 am French class, we began to hear muffled banging noises coming from somewhere outside of our classroom.

As soon as our teacher went to investigate the sounds, she slammed the door shut and told us to get under our desks and for someone to call 911. I took out my phone and, as I later found out, placed the only call to the police by someone in the building. The next 10-minute period was the longest 10-minute period of my entire life. It felt like hours.

From the floor in the back of my classroom, I took one glance at the front of the room where my teacher had stood and instead saw a man with two holsters over his shoulders begin to turn towards me and down my aisle of desks. I never saw his face. I had nowhere to escape and no time to react or even think. As I turned my head back, I told the voice on the other end of the phone that he was here, but I still didn't totally understand what that meant. The only decision that I was left with was to act as if I was already dead.

The force of the first bullet caused me to throw the phone from my hand and it landed next to the head of a girl named Emily. She picked it up and remained on the call with the police the entire time. Emily was ultimately able to give the dispatcher his location and help the SWAT team to get to us.

What was once a set of seemingly unusual bangs had now became a constant thunder of gunfire. It would pause momentarily while he changed out his extended ammunition magazines. The intensity of those sounds did vary slightly while he traveled back and forth between the three rooms. There were also screams in the beginning but generally nobody really saying anything.

Each time he came back into our room I was shot again. The second and third time in both my hips and the fourth time through my right shoulder. I don't ever remember thinking I was going to die however. I just kept thinking that I couldn't believe this was really happening to me. It was so surreal. There were times I felt like I was almost dreaming.

Cho's mental health records should have disqualified him from purchasing firearms.

But this dream was finally interrupted by silence. As quickly as everything started, it all just stopped. By this point you could hear the police were very close. I thought he was hiding in our room and waiting to engage them when they entered. But as soon as the police came into our room I heard them say, "Shooter down," and realized that he had committed suicide in the front of our classroom. I then heard the EMT's begin their triage and they said, "This one's yellow, this one's red" then "black tag, black tag, black tag." This is when I knew some of my classmates were dead.

I put one hand up on a desk to let them know I was alive. They marked me as yellow, dragged me out into the hallway, and it was there that I began the long road to recovery.

Today, I still carry 3 bullets with me and a newly implanted titanium rod in my body.

The fact is, Congressmen, I wouldn't be sitting in front of you today if it wasn't for that 10-minute experience that changed my life.

I wouldn't be sitting in front of you today if it weren't for the phone call I made and the exceptional work of the law enforcement agencies that responded.

Ineffective and Unenforceable Gun Laws

And finally, as simply as I can put it, I wouldn't be sitting in front of you today if our federal gun laws had been stronger. If Seung-Hui Cho, who had a known mental health history that disqualified him from purchasing firearms, had had his record uploaded to the NICS [National Instant Check System] background check system as required, I wouldn't be here in front of you today. The existing federal law at the time was too weak to protect me and my classmates, as it was intended to do.

So the fact is, I shouldn't be sitting in front of you today.

When we learned that fact, that Cho's mental health records should have disqualified him from purchasing firearms through the legal way he did, we worked with Congress to help ensure that states were getting more records uploaded into the National Instant Check System (NICS). This was a good first step, however it should be known that this improvement has yet to be applied in every state. This weakness then opened my eyes to the greater patchwork of state and federal laws in our country. And what I learned surprised me.

I bought an AK-47 without showing any ID or going through any background check.

What I learned was that many of our state and federal gun laws are written in ways to make them ineffective and unenforceable. Even if Cho had been properly turned down during a background check from the gun dealer, he could have easily attended any of the dozens of gun shows that take place throughout Virginia each weekend and bought the same weapons from a "private seller" with no background check into his mental history, and no questions asked. I know this first hand, and I tried to demonstrate it all to you with the video that you just saw. The existing Brady Act [system of background checks for gun purchases passed in 1993], as it is written, is too weak to protect future Americans from another Seung-Hui Cho or other prohibited purchasers.

Last summer, I traveled all over the country visiting gun shows in an attempt to expose the Gun Show Loophole. I passed right by all the licensed dealers responsibly conducting background checks and went right through the loophole over and over again. I went to shows in Texas, Ohio, Maine, Minnesota and right across the river in my home state of Virginia. I was amazed at how quick and easy it was getting my hands on just about any type of weapon I could imagine.

I bought, or watched a friend buy, 9mm's, 22's, Tech-9's, and Mack-11's. I bought an AK-47 without showing any ID or going through any background check. I even bought the same type of gun that shot me. Each transaction took less than 5 minutes. And when I was done, either I, or the purchaser I went with, would turn all weapons over to the police. The sickening thing about what I did and the footage you just saw was that everything was completely legal under our current law.

I can think of NO reasonable, responsible, logical reason why that should be. I can think of no reason why the Gun Show Loophole should exist. Why should sellers at one table be required to run background checks, when the sellers, literally two tables down—with the exact same weapons—are allowed to sell their guns to anyone who just has the cash in hand? The reasonable, responsible answer is: They shouldn't.

The Importance of Closing the Gun Show Loophole

It's no mystery why the guns sold by so-called "private sellers" are often more expensive than the exact same model sold by licensed gun dealers. Purchasers who know they can't pass a background check are willing to pay a premium. One seller told me straight up, and I quote, "No paperwork, no tax, that's gotta be worth something." For gun traffickers, domestic abusers and felons who can't pass a background check, that's worth plenty.

It is far too easy for dangerous people to get hands on dangerous weapons.

The fact is, since the Brady Act began requiring background checks only on licensed dealers, it has denied, and thus prevented, more than 2 million firearms from falling into the hands of dangerous prohibited purchasers. So it's only logical that this number would increase if the background check is further applied to private sellers dealing guns at gun shows because everyone knows that's an easy way to get around it.

My personal experiences provide ample evidence as to why our federal gun laws need to be strengthened. Getting more records into the NICS system is absolutely important. But without applying these records on a broader scale, that means without, at least, applying the background check to private sellers at public gun shows, all the new records in the world aren't really any more useful. And I'm here to tell you, first-hand, that ineffective laws that put guns in the hands of the wrong people are a serious threat to the public safety of your citizens. My experiences since April 16, 2007, have lead me to conclude that it is far too easy for dangerous people to get their hands on dangerous weapons in this country. So today, the gun show loophole must be closed.

The fact is, Congressmen, I wouldn't be sitting here in front of you today if I didn't believe, with every part of me, that this is the right thing to do.

I wouldn't be sitting here in front of you today if I didn't know that closing the Gun Show Loophole will save American lives.

And finally, I wouldn't be sitting here in front of you today if I didn't believe that my elected officials will do what is reasonable and right to protect their citizens.

7

An Updated Background Check System Will Help Prevent Gun Violence

Mayors Against Illegal Guns

Formed in 2006, Mayors Against Illegal Guns is a coalition of over 550 mayors who support reforms to fight illegal gun trafficking and gun violence in the United States, while still respecting the Second Amendment.

The background check system designed by Congress in 1993 to prohibit dangerous people from purchasing guns is not working effectively. But with the enforcement of critical new regulations, the National Instant Criminal Background Check System (NICS) could be an effective tool in preventing gun violence. One such regulation would require the names of all people known to be dangerous or criminal be registered in the NICS database, and those names should be referenced every time a gun is purchased.

In 1968, assassins gunned down Martin Luther King, Jr. and Robert F. Kennedy. In the wake of that double tragedy, Congress passed the first federal laws to limit access to guns, by prohibiting dangerous people, like felons, drug abusers, and the mentally ill from purchasing or possessing guns.

In 1993, Congress passed the Brady Bill, named for President [Ronald] Reagan's press secretary James Brady, who had been critically wounded in the assassination attempt on President Reagan. The Brady Bill created a system of background checks that helped to make real the purpose of the 1968 law.

The System Is Broken

Unfortunately, incomplete records and loopholes in the law have stopped background checks from doing their job:

- The Columbine [Colorado, April 20, 1999] killers got around the system by using guns bought at a gun show from an unlicensed seller: no paperwork, no questions asked.

- At Virginia Tech [Virginia, April 16, 2007], a killer got a gun he should have been prohibited from buying because his records were never reported to the FBI's gun background check system.

- The shooter in Tucson [Arizona, January 8, 2011] also got a gun he should have been prohibited from buying because his records weren't in the database—and then got a second gun because lax federal regulations frustrated the intent of the law.

Most murders that take place with illegal guns do not make the headlines. Every day, 34 Americans are murdered with guns, and most of them are possessed illegally. Since 1968, more than 400,000 Americans have been killed with guns.

The system needs to be fixed. Creating a comprehensive system to keep guns out of the hands of dangerous people requires two steps:

Step one: Get all the names of people who should be prohibited from buying a gun into the background check system.

Step two: Close the loopholes in the background check system by requiring a background check for every gun sale.

STEP ONE: Get All the Names of People Who Should Be Prohibited from Buying a Gun into the Background Check System.

Context: NICS, the National Instant Criminal Background Check System, which is used to conduct background checks on prospective gun buyers, is missing millions of records. Federal law requires records concerning the mentally ill, drug abusers, perpetrators of domestic violence, and other people who are forbidden, under current state and federal law, from having guns to be included in the system. The problem of missing records became obvious in 2007, when Seung Hui Cho, who was prohibited from owning a gun due to mental illness, was not listed in the background check system and was therefore able to buy two guns to commit the Virginia Tech massacre. Congress responded by passing the NICS Improvement Amendments Act [in 2008], which encourages states to share records. As a result, the number of records in NICS' Mental Defective File increased significantly under the new law, from nearly 300,000 in 2006 to more than 1.1 million today. The murders in Tucson, however, show that problems persist. The shooter, Jared Loughner, was able to buy a shotgun less than a year after admitting to the U.S. Army that he was a regular drug abuser because the armed forces had not forwarded his name to NICS. Today, there are just over 2,000 people listed as drug abusers in NICS.

Revised legislation would strengthen the NICS system in six ways:

Funding: Fully fund the NICS Improvement Amendments Act to help agencies and states cover the costs of gathering records and making them electronically available to the FBI.

The legislation, enacted in 2008, is failing to achieve its goals in part because Congress has supplied only 5.3% of the authorized amount from Fiscal Year 2009 through Fiscal Year 2011. That money was supposed to be available to states to help cover the cost of gathering and supplying records.

The revised law would guarantee full funding to states and federal agencies to comply with reporting requirements to the NICS database.

Penalties: Establish tougher penalties for states that do not comply with the law by cutting more of their Justice Department funding.

The NICS Improvement Amendments Act establishes only minor penalties for non-compliance. It sets out a timeline, and in each year starting in Fiscal Year 2011 states are required to turn over a target percentage of the records they have naming people who should not be allowed to buy guns under federal law. If they do not comply, they could face cuts to a portion of their federal justice assistance funding. The potential cuts are small, however: only 3% to 5% of a single grant (Byrne Justice Assistance Grants or JAG), which provides about $300 million a year nationwide to states. Furthermore, DOJ [Department of Justice] has almost total discretion to reduce or waive them.

Federal agencies are not following the law.

Revised legislation would put in place tighter deadlines and stricter penalties for states to comply with the law and submit records. States would be required to turn over 75% of their records within two years of enactment and 90% of their records within six years or they would face cuts not only to JAG grants, but also to other Justice Department programs that normally guarantee a share to each state, such as the State Criminal Alien Assistance Program (SCAAP, $249 million a year); Title II grants for juvenile justice ($60 million a year); Juvenile Accountability Block Grants (JABG, $46 million a year), and Enforcing Underage Drinking Laws Block Grants ($20 million a year). Furthermore, these penalties would rise to 50% of each grant.

Why it matters: Across the country, the total potential penalties that face all states combined under the current NICS Improvement Amendments Act are only about $15 million.

Federal reporting: Require every federal agency to certify to the Attorney General twice a year that all relevant records have been submitted.

Under the NICS Improvement Amendments Act, each Federal agency must provide to DOJ, at least quarterly, the name of any person it is aware is federally prohibited from buying guns. Current law does not, however, hold any person accountable for guaranteeing an agency's compliance. And federal agencies are not following the law. For example, only three agencies have sent any records on drug abusers to the FBI.

Revised legislation would hold agencies accountable for quarterly reporting by requiring the head of each agency to report to the Attorney General, twice a year, about the number of records it has shared in each category of prohibited person. Each report would include the agency head's written certification that all relevant records have been transmitted.

Why it matters: Even though Jared Loughner admitted to the U.S. Army that he regularly abused drugs, the Army did not submit his name to the FBI for inclusion in NICS as required by law, and less than a year later, Loughner was able to pass a background check and buy a shotgun. Later, Loughner bought the Glock he used to kill six people and injure 13 others.

Mental health definitions: Clarify the definition of mentally ill people who are prohibited from having guns to ensure that dangerous people are included in NICS.

Two critical changes are needed to ensure that people who are mentally ill are listed in NICS. First, the system should include people who have been suspended or expelled from a federally funded college or university because of mental illness. Second, it should include people who are compelled by a court to take medication for mental illness or to get other mental health care, even if they are not "committed" to in-patient treatment, as the ATF [Bureau of Alcohol, Tobacco, Firearms, and Explosives] currently interprets the law.

Why it matters: Jared Loughner was deemed too mentally ill to come to school without a note from a mental health professional, but safe enough to buy a gun.

Drug abuse definitions: Clarify the definition of drug abusers who are prohibited from having guns to ensure that dangerous people are included in NICS.

Since 1968, federal law has prohibited anyone "who is an unlawful user of or addicted to any controlled substance" from possessing any gun. The revised law would do two things to enforce that prohibition. First, it would reverse the overly narrow interpretation that ATF and the FBI now give to the law. They interpret it to apply only to people who have had a drug-related arrest, a drug-related conviction, a failed drug test, or an admission of drug use within the previous year. The revised law would change that one-year prohibition to a five-year prohibition. Second, the revised law would require federal courts to report to NICS anyone sentenced to mandatory drug treatment even if the requirement was part of a diversionary program that does not result in conviction.

Due process: Safeguard the rights of people who are listed in NICS.

The revised legislation would continue to ensure that individuals who were wrongly included in NICS as a prohibited purchaser are able to seek relief and be removed from the list of prohibited gun purchasers. For example, those who were arrested on a drug charge within the past five years but can show they have recovered from their addiction would be able to regain their gun rights. So would people who had been mentally ill but have recovered and no longer present a risk.

Step Two: Close the Loopholes in the Background Check System by Requiring a Background Check for Every Gun Sale.

Context: Even if the NICS database included the name of every person prohibited from having a gun under federal or state law, it would still be easy and legal to obtain guns with no background check, no questions asked. That is because the current law only applies to gun sales by federally licensed dealers.

The new law would require that non-licensed people selling guns ensure that the buyer has undergone a background check in NICS.

Under current federal law, only persons "engaged in the business" of selling guns are required to get a license, keep paperwork, and conduct background checks. People who maintain they are collectors or only occasionally sell guns are not required to do these checks. Such sellers often congregate at gun shows, which is why many refer to this exception as the "gun show loophole." But felons can exploit the loophole whether they are at a gun show or not—buying guns with no background checks at unlicensed sellers' homes, via classified ads, or even in some cases on the internet. Experts estimate that over six million guns a year—perhaps 40% of all sales— are made by unlicensed private dealers not subject to the law.

Background checks:

The new law would require that non-licensed people selling guns ensure that the buyer has undergone a background check in NICS. Sellers would be able to do so in three ways. First, the seller can go to a licensed dealer to have a background check run on the buyer. The revised law would cap the fee for conducting these background checks on behalf of private sellers at $15. Second, the seller can inspect a permit issued to the buyer by a state or local government that confirms they have passed a background check within the previous five years. Third, the seller can go to or contact a law enforcement official for the background check at the time of purchase.

Why it matters: ATF has reported that over 27% of the guns involved in its criminal trafficking investigations were tied to trafficking by unlicensed sellers, and over 30% were tied to trafficking at gun shows.

Reasonable exceptions:

Similar to the Brady Law, revised legislation would exempt certain gun permittees and some types of transactions from background checks:

- Sales to a federally licensed dealer, manufacturer or wholesaler (including sales of curio or relic firearms to a licensed collectors);

- Sales to law enforcement;

- Transfers of guns to an immediate family member, grandchild, or grandparent;

- Inheritance of guns; and

- Sharing guns while hunting, at a shooting range, or at a competition.

8

Students Should Have the Right to Carry Guns on College Campuses

David Burnett

David Burnett is the director of public relations for Students for Concealed Carry on Campus (SCCC), a national, non-partisan, grassroots organization that supports the legalization of concealed carry by licensed individuals on college campuses.

The mass murder that occurred in April 2007 at Virginia Polytechnic Institute and State University is just one example of the many college shooting sprees in which students and teachers were unable to defend themselves because their campuses were mandated gun-free zones. Gun-free zones are supposed to be safe areas, but statistics show that campuses are not always safe. And the fact is the only people who truly benefit from such designated zones are criminals and killers. Students and teachers have the right to defend themselves, and if they are responsible enough to apply for and receive a license to carry a concealed firearm, no law should deny them that right.

It was nothing less than a morning of sheer terror.

If you asked any student on the quiet campus of Virginia Tech [Virginia Polytechnic Institute and State University] on the morning of April 16, 2007, most would have told you they

David Burnett, "Colleges Reveal Their Plan to Keep Students from Becoming Victims of On-Campus Violence: Duck & Cover," National Rifle Association Online, June 28, 2010. NRAILA.org. Copyright © 2010 by David Burnett. All rights reserved. Reproduced by permission.

felt safe. As they gathered their backpacks, pencils and textbooks and prepared to go about their day, no one imagined the sleepy town of Blacksburg, Va., would be the stage for the worst college shooting in U.S. history.

One of the students feeling particularly safe that morning was a mentally disturbed youth—he would want his name to be printed here, but we won't—whose plans differed radically from those of his classmates. Instead of textbooks and calculators, his plan involved two handguns and 400 rounds of ammunition.

Gun-Free Zones Are Not Necessarily Safe Zones

Despite his psychological problems, he showed deliberate and calculated strategy in selecting his target. There's no doubt he felt safe planning and carrying out his attack, since just the previous year Virginia Tech officials "heroically" defeated a bill allowing lawful concealed carry on campus. The officials were jubilant at their victory, certain that the bill's defeat would help students "feel safe." They realized too late that feeling safe and being safe were two different things—the bill's failure guaranteed that no one was capable of resisting an armed killer.

Walking into a dormitory, the shooter began by gunning down two students. It took two hours before officials alerted students to the murders. During that interval, police arrived and began investigating, the killer mailed videotaped rants and a manifesto to NBC, and Virginia Tech officials privately warned their own families and secured their own offices. What school officials didn't do, however, was warn students that their safety that morning might be in jeopardy, as required by federal law. A review by the U.S. Department of Education released in May [2010] found that Virginia Tech failed to take prompt action in warning the campus community of the possibility of danger after the bodies of the two students were found, in accordance with a mandate called the Clery Act.

More than two hours later, with police still on campus, the perpetrator entered Norris Hall and began murdering more students. One survivor later stated that the total randomness of the killing was still hard to get over; without the ability to resist, the choice of life or death rested solely in the hands of a mentally deranged killer. Eventually, realizing armed officers were approaching, he took one final life—his own.

In nine minutes he fired 174 shots, killed 32 people and wounded 15—traumatizing a whole campus and leaving an entire nation to grieve. Although the massacre was devastating, it could have been far worse: The killer missed with 73 percent of his shots, and he had more than 200 rounds remaining.

The Virginia Tech story is familiar to anyone who followed the news in 2007. Killing sprees aren't new, but it was the first time in decades that a college campus was hit, or that so many died.

College campuses represent one of the final frontiers in the fight for concealed carry.

What is less well known is that there have been more than a dozen other college shootings since Virginia Tech. You probably didn't hear about most of them because there wasn't enough blood to earn a cover story, but each of these attacks had one thing in common. They all occurred under the same banner: "gun-free zone."

Colleges fight hard for these "gun-free" zones, wearing them as a badge of honor. They even advertise their campuses as being defense-free.

As Right-to-Carry freedoms have expanded in recent years, such legally sanctioned victim disarmament zones have dwindled. State legislators and average Americans are realizing that gun-free zones appeal to only two groups of people: the irrational, unreasonable anti-gun crowd . . . and killers.

College campuses represent one of the final frontiers in the fight for concealed carry.

A Movement Against Defenselessness

In many ways, this is one of the most vital battles. It is here, under the careful tutelage of mostly left-leaning professors, that the best and brightest are challenging their worldviews and forming new ones. And it is here that students are deluded into believing that they are safer when disarmed. The future is being fashioned in these classrooms, and it doesn't bode well for America's freedoms.

But there is hope. A new generation of freedom's defenders is rising up to take a stand for its rights, and demanding an end to discrimination against law-abiding armed citizens.

Students for Concealed Carry on Campus (SCCC) was formed in direct response to the Virginia Tech shootings. The group's goal? Stop pretending a piece of paper taped to the door will stop a killer.

Originally, the group started out on the social networking site Facebook. But after another psychopathic killing spree at Northern Illinois University, the group began receiving national attention. Suddenly major news agencies were investigating whether Right-to-Carry could deter killers at colleges. Group membership quickly blossomed into more than 40,000 supporters.

The organization began holding "empty holster protest" events at colleges nationwide. As a symbol of their forced defenselessness, students strapped on empty holsters while attending class. The most recent protest in April included thousands of students at more than 130 colleges.

Educational activities such as concealed carry classes, gun safety lessons or other firearms training are held at some schools. Other members sponsor debates, speaking events or free days at the range for professors.

For the first time in the history of the gun rights movement, the youth of America are stepping up to take the lead.

Colleges' responses have proven interesting. Many turn deaf ears to students lobbying for their rights. Others have shown they're no longer content to tread on just one amendment.

In Texas, some students were forbidden from wearing empty holsters on campus, until a federal judge stepped in and enforced their right to free speech.

In Michigan, some professors wanted to cancel classes, based only on their fear of empty holsters.

In Kentucky, despite a workplace protection law allowing employees to keep guns in cars without reprisal, one university fired a graduate student for having a handgun locked in his car on campus property. The car, incidentally, was parked more than a mile away while the student was busy saving lives in the university hospital emergency room.

The criticisms of allowing guns on campus fly fast and thick:

- Guns and alcohol don't mix.

- Students aren't responsible enough.

- Guns will lead to more violence.

Such criticisms come not just from the hackneyed gun-ban crowd, but from the "enlightened" university officials and campus police chiefs. Somehow, opponents of campus carry believe responsible adults with concealed carry permits are actually dormant criminals, just waiting for the law to sanction guns on campus before cutting loose with sprees of violent crime.

It's definitely not the story they tell when advertising their colleges or soliciting donations.

Concealed Carry Works When Given the Chance

Despite the heavy-handed opposition of colleges and anti-gun groups (who accused SCCC of being another arm of the so-called "gun lobby"), the protests drew the attention of state legislators.

Since 2007, 22 states have considered legislation allowing lawful concealed carry on campus. While many of these bills stalled in committee, Arizona, South Carolina and Georgia passed laws at least allowing guns to be kept in parked cars on campus. (Note that most colleges ban guns in cars, daring to extend their authority even to commuting students' drives to and from the schools).

Presently, 25 states ban guns on college campuses, eight of them leave it to universities to set their rules, and some states don't address the issue at all, which sometimes creates legal gray areas.

As usual, the ignorant criticisms of expanding Right-to-Carry fall flat when compared to reality. Every public university in Utah has allowed concealed handguns on campus since 2006, with no misfires, accidental shootings or incidents of any kind reported. Likewise, Blue Ridge Community College in Virginia has allowed concealed carry on campus for years with zero complaints.

Guns became permissible on some campuses in Michigan in 2009 when law enforcement officials refused to enforce Michigan State University's non-binding ban on weapons. The school changed its policy to reflect state law, which prohibits concealed carry only in dorms, stadiums and classrooms.

But perhaps the greatest illustration of the difference between victim disarmament and victim empowerment—and its effect on crime—is found in Colorado.

Two schools stand in stark contrast on the issue. After Colorado became a shall-issue Right-to-Carry state in 2003, Colorado State University (CSU) chose to comply with the law and allow concealed carry on campus. Though certainly there are other factors at play, the school's crime rate has steadily declined ever since, dropping from 800 crimes in 2002 to 200 in 2008. Sexual offenses alone dropped from 47 in 2002 to only two in 2008. James Alderden, the county sheriff and a gun rights supporter, reports absolutely no problems from permit-holders.

Meanwhile, the University of Colorado (CU), which banned guns, has experienced a dramatic increase in crime. In contrast to CSU's 61 percent drop in the last five years, CU crime is up 37 percent.

The data show that concealed carry works as a deterrent on a college campus.

Shockingly, citing "risks" of allowing guns on campus, CSU moved to ban concealed carry on campus in the spring of 2010—despite hundreds of students petitioning against the ban, and a near-unanimous vote from student government. Sheriff Alderden vehemently opposed the unconstitutional ban, declaring his jail off-limits to anyone arresting lawfully armed students, and vowing to testify in defense of anyone prosecuted for being armed.

Just before press time, under pressure from SCCC, CSU announced it would rescind its planned prohibition on concealed carry, leaving students there better able to defend themselves against criminals. More than a dozen other community colleges in Colorado subsequently changed their policies to allow concealed carry on campus.

College Students Deserve the Right to Defend Themselves

Clearly the data show that concealed carry works as a deterrent on a college campus. Yet even some gun owners think back to their college days, picture their sons or daughters on a campus full of students and question the wisdom of allowing concealed weapons on campus. Despite the knowledge that anyone carrying a firearm would already have to meet several stringent requirements to possess a permit, some pro-gun parents even question if such a proposal is too dangerous.

The better question to ponder is, isn't it too dangerous not to allow concealed carry? Gun-free zones only serve to protect killers by ensuring they will face no resistance.

College campuses may be safer than the average city, but that doesn't mean they're safe. Statistics show there are nine sexual assaults per day on campuses nationwide. Imagine your loved one, perhaps a son or daughter, sitting in a classroom targeted by a killer. Or picture your daughter, niece or granddaughter walking home from the library late at night and being ambushed by a serial rapist. Colleges must be held accountable for forcing these victims to be disarmed and helpless as a condition of admittance.

[Students] are boldly insisting that colleges get serious about safety and stop pretending signs and rules will protect them.

Colleges often argue that "kids" aren't responsible enough to carry a gun—a senseless argument since most state laws don't authorize concealed carry until the age of 21. These "kids" can drive a car at 16 and get married, get a mortgage and join the military at 18. There's something backward when the same "kids" who defend our nation with M16s are somehow too dangerous to carry .38s for self-defense on college campuses.

The fact that taxpayer-funded colleges can force Right-to-Carry permit holders to surrender their Second Amendment rights upon crossing the invisible (and unsecured) borders of their campuses should anger every sensible American.

Police took nine minutes to reach the Virginia Tech killer. Northern Illinois University police took two minutes to confront the attacker at their school. And at the University of Alabama (Huntsville), where a Harvard-trained professor is accused of shooting six of her colleagues, the campus police station was literally next door to the site of the murder. Nevertheless, police could not prevent these crimes.

When a college doesn't secure its borders and the students' only alternatives for responding to attacks include huddling together (presenting the best possible target for a murderer), dialing 9-1-1 and playing dead, something is indeed wrong and has to change.

These students need—and deserve—your help. Braving the wrath of the academic class, they are boldly insisting that colleges get serious about safety and stop pretending signs and rules will protect them. With minimal funding and maximum efforts, student activists have brought the issue to national exposure, called out the vulnerability and inaction of colleges, and successfully prompted legislation to be heard in nearly half the states in the union.

This battle isn't just for student rights—it's for the rights of every single American. Our future is being shaped in these classrooms. We must continue the fight to ensure that future is bright, safe and free.

9

Students Should Not Be Allowed to Carry Guns on College Campuses

Darby Dickerson

Darby Dickerson, dean of Texas Tech University School of Law, is an expert in higher education law and policy and is an elected member of the American Law Institute. Her scholarly articles have appeared in legal journals across the country.

The shootings that have occurred in recent years at US colleges and universities have generated passionate debate about how best to prevent such violence and whether persons should be allowed to carry concealed guns on campuses. Various experts, such as Jesus Villahermosa, a Washington state SWAT officer and founder of Crisis Reality Training, believe there is no credible evidence that students or staff carrying guns would reduce crime. In fact, research has shown that the brains of most college students have not fully developed with regard to impulse control and judgment; therefore, allowing students access to guns could actually increase reckless shooting incidents.

Colleges and universities occupy a special place in American society. They are much more than a series of buildings and collection of individuals. Instead, they are dynamic living and learning environments where individuals with varying levels of maturity interact, often under stressful circumstances. While recognizing the right of responsible individuals to possess firearms under other circumstances, the unique characteristics of a university campus make the presence of firearms problematic. . . .

National Context Regarding Guns on Campuses

Currently, 26 states plus the District of Columbia ban concealed weapons on college and university property. Twenty-three states allow individual campuses to decide. Only Utah allows guns on the campuses at public institutions; the state allows private institutions to set their own policies.

In November 2008, the American Association of State Colleges and Universities issued a higher-education policy brief titled "Concealed Weapons on State College Campuses: In Pursuit of Individual Liberty and Collective Security." The organization aptly framed the issue of guns on campus as follows:

> The tragic events at Virginia Tech [April 2007] and Northern Illinois University [February 2008] have policymakers, campus officials and citizens looking for solutions to prevent future attacks. Violent shootings that have occurred on a few college campuses in recent years have provoked a debate over the best ways to ensure the safety of students, faculty and staff. Lawmakers in several states have advanced the idea allowing citizens with concealed weapons permits to carry their weapons on campus. . . . These legislative proposals have been met with considerable controversy, evoking strong emotion on both sides. Thus far, Utah is the only state to have adopted this policy. All other state legislatures where similar bills have been introduced have rejected the idea.

> The Second Amendment—the right to keep and bear arms as established by the U.S. Constitution and many state constitutions—is not at issue in this controversy. Rather, this is a policy debate over how best to ensure public safety, as the

Second Amendment is subject to reasonable restrictions, such as bans on guns in schools. The majority opinion of the U.S. Supreme Court recently concluded in *District of Columbia vs. Heller*:

Although we do not undertake an exhaustive historical analysis today of the full scope of the Second Amendment, nothing in our opinion should be taken to cast doubt on longstanding prohibitions on the possession of firearms by felons and the mentally ill, or laws forbidding the carrying of firearms in *sensitive places such as schools and government buildings* [emphasis added], or laws imposing conditions and qualifications on the commercial sale of arms.

The majority also noted: "We identify these presumptively lawful regulatory measures only as examples; our list does not purport to be exhaustive." While striking down the District of Columbia's strict ban on handguns, the justices did not call into question any of the existing gun bans on college campuses.

The most recent published case regarding guns on campus was issued by the Virginia Supreme Court on January 13, 2011. In *Digiacinto v. Rector & Visitors of George Mason University*, a visitor to the public university claimed that the university's policy prohibiting possession of firearms on campus violated his constitutional rights. Relying on the conclusion in *Heller* that the right to keep and bear arms is not absolute, the court held that the Second Amendment does not prevent the government from prohibiting firearms in sensitive places, such as George Mason's campus and events.

In determining that the university was a "sensitive place" under *Heller*, the court relied on the parties' stipulation that George Mason has 30,000 students enrolled ranging from age 16 to senior citizens, that more than 350 incoming freshman would be under 18, that elementary and high school students attend summer camps on campus, and that children attend an on-campus preschool. All of these individuals use George

Mason's buildings and attend on-campus events. The court also emphasized that "[u]nlike a public street or park, a university traditionally has not been open to the general public, 'but instead is an institute of higher learning that is devoted to its mission of public education.' . . . Moreover, parents who send their children to a university have a reasonable expectation that the university will maintain a campus free of foreseeable harm."

In October 2010, the Colorado Supreme Court granted certiorari [review] in *Regents of the University of Colorado v. Students for Concealed Carry on Campus, LLC* to consider "[w]hether the General Assembly intended the Concealed Carry Act to divest the Board of Regents of its constitutional and statutory authority to enact safety and welfare measures for the University of Colorado's campuses" and "[w]hether a constitutional challenge to a statute or ordinance regulating the right to bear arms is governed by the deferential rational basis standard of review or a more stringent reasonable exercise standard of review." In the underlying case, a student-interest group sued the university alleging that its weapons control policy violated Colorado's Concealed Carry Act (CCA) and the right to bear arms in self-defense under the Colorado Constitution. Although the trial court dismissed the claims, the Colorado Court of Appeals reversed and remanded for further proceedings. The case does not yet appear on the state supreme court's public oral-argument calendar.

Concern About Violence on College Campuses

The tragedies at Virginia Tech, Northern Illinois, Appalachian School of Law [January 2002], and the University of Alabama in Huntsville [February 2010], among others, illustrate that our campuses are not immune from violence. Studies reflect that violence on campus is most commonly perpetrated by students, against students. In response to the Virginia Tech shooting, the U.S. Secret Service, Department of Education, and F.B.I. studied violence at institutions of higher education. As part of this study, 272 incidents of targeted violence were identified through a comprehensive search of open-source reports from 1900 to 2008. The incidents include various forms of targeted violence, ranging from domestic violence to mass murder. Most incidents occurred during the 1990s and 2000s. Across these 272 incidents, the perpetrators killed 281 people and injured 247 more. The perpetrators used guns 54% of the time, knives or bladed instruments 21% of the time, and a combination of weapons 10% of the time. Florida had the fourth highest number of incidents in the study.

Concealed carry laws have the potential to dramatically increase violence on college and university campuses.

In 2008, the International Association of Campus Law Enforcement Administrators, Inc. (IACLEA) issued a statement in response to various state legislative initiatives to allow persons to carry concealed weapons on college and university campuses. Below are excerpts from the IACLEA statement:

IACLEA's Board of Directors believes "concealed carry" initiatives do not make campuses safer. There is no credible evidence to suggest that the presence of students carrying concealed weapons would reduce violence on our college campuses.

- There is no credible statistical evidence demonstrating that laws allowing the carrying of concealed firearms reduce crime. In fact, the evidence suggests that permissive concealed carry laws generally will increase crime. . . .

- Use of a gun in self-defense appears to be a rare occurrence. For example, of the 30,694 Americans who died by gunfire in 2005, only 147 were killed by firearms in justifiable homicides by private citizens. . . .

IACLEA is concerned that concealed carry laws have the potential to dramatically increase violence on college and university campuses that our Members are empowered to protect. Among the concerns with concealed carry laws or policies are: the potential for accidental discharge or misuse of firearms at on-campus or off-campus parties where large numbers of students are gathered or at student gatherings where alcohol or drugs are being consumed, as well as the potential for guns to be used as a means to settle disputes between or among students. There is also a real concern that campus police officers responding to a situation involving an active shooter may not be able to distinguish between the shooter and others with firearms.

• Public safety is threatened by student gun owners. One study found that two-thirds of gun-owning college students engage in binge drinking. Gun-owning students are more likely than unarmed college students to drink "frequently and excessively" and then engage in risky activities, such as driving when under the influence of alcohol, vandalizing property, and getting into trouble with police. . . .

• Another study similarly discovered that college student gun owners are more likely than those who do not own guns to engage in activities that put themselves and others at risk for severe or life-threatening injuries, including reckless behavior involving alcohol, driving while intoxicated, and suffering an alcohol-related injury. . . .

Suicides accounted for 55 percent of the nation's nearly 31,000 firearms deaths in 2005, the most recent year statistics are available from the Center for Disease Control and Prevention. . . . Public Health researchers have concluded that in homes where guns are present, the likelihood that someone in the home will die from suicide or homicide is much greater.

We urge public policy makers to weigh heavily the concerns of IACLEA regarding the unintended consequences of any proposals to allow college students and any other persons to carry concealed weapons on campus. We believe that the research we have cited shows that these unintended consequences include:

1. Likely increase in reckless shooting incidents resulting in injuries and deaths from firearms on campus;

2. Likely increase in both homicides and suicides;

3. Increased exposure of campus police to injuries;

4. Unfunded mandates resulting from policy changes, including resources necessary to investigate firearms incidents, thefts of firearms, and checking for underage/ prohibited possessors. . . .

Restricting Guns on Campus

The work of Jesus Villahermosa, founder of Crisis Realty Training and a S.W.A.T. officer in Washington State, also reflects the wisdom of restricting guns on campus. Officer Villahermosa has first-hand experience responding to gun-related violence in schools. In an essay published in the *Chronicle of Higher Education*, he concluded:

> I have been a deputy sheriff for more than 26 years and was the first certified master defensive-tactics instructor for law-enforcement personnel in the state of Washington. In addition, I have been a firearms instructor and for several decades have served on my county sheriff's SWAT team, where I am now point man on the entry team. Given my extensive experience dealing with violence in the workplace and at schools and colleges, I do not think professors and administrators, let alone students, should carry guns. . . .

Many universities with policies prohibiting guns on campus also realize that at least some of their students may own and want to use guns for club sports or recreational hunting; these universities have developed policies and procedures to allow students to register and store rifles and other weapons traditionally used in sport in a locked vault maintained by campus police. . . .

Universities that otherwise prohibit weapons on campus have also developed policies to account for R.O.T.C. programs and law-enforcement officers taking courses or attending programs on campus. . . .

Adding a weapon . . . into the mix can quickly turn a constructive meeting into one filled with fear and intimidation.

Although legislation to permit open-carry of weapons is or recently has been pending in a few states, including Arizona, Arkansas, Oklahoma, Texas, and Utah, no legislature to date has authorized open-carry on college or university campuses. In states where open-carry legislation has been debated, university faculty and presidents have expressed concerns for their own safety and the nature of the academic environment. This fear is understandable, especially since faculty members must often interact with students who may be disappointed in their evaluations and grades. Engaging in difficult, but necessary, conversations with students to help them develop professionally and personally can be challenging under normal circumstances, but adding a weapon—especially one displayed openly—into the mix can quickly turn a constructive meeting into one filled with fear and intimidation.

Brain Development Studies

Although most traditional-age college students appear to be physically mature, their brains are still developing. Over the past decade, researchers have discovered that the human brain changes significantly during adolescence—often defined as the second decade of life—and is not fully developed until about 24.

The areas of the brain that develop last include the prefrontal cortex. Described as the "CEO of the body," this area "allows us to prioritize thoughts, imagine, think in the abstract *anticipate consequences, plan, and control impulses.*" Because the brain develops back to front, "judgment" is last to mature. As Dr. Ken Winters of the University of Minnesota has explained, "By age 18, the adolescent's judgment for *structured challenges* is roughly equal to that of adults. But judgment that *involves resisting impulses or delaying gratification* is still under construction during late adolescence and early adulthood."

Accessibility to guns and other weapons ... is likely to lead to additional incidents of self-injury, accidental shootings, and homicides.

From these new studies, we have learned that, as a general rule, individuals in their late teens and early 20s:

- prefer physical activities;

- prefer high-excitement and low-effort activities;

- prefer novelty;

- exhibit poor planning and judgment;

- often fail to consider negative consequences of their actions; and

- seek riskier, impulsive behaviors.

Therefore, conduct most adults perceive as dangerous and risky, they perceive as fun. In addition, some evidence exists that "being in a group accentuates risk taking," which has tremendous implications for student affairs professionals. Moreover, the research underscores that alcohol and other drug use not only impedes brain development, but can have long-term negative consequences on brain structure.

High-risk alcohol and other drug use among our student populations represent the number one risk for our students. This is true even for students who do not drink or take drugs, as they can—and frequently are—the victims of others' abuse. The grim statistics include:

- 1,700 college students between the ages of 18 and 24 die each year from alcohol-related unintentional injuries, including motor vehicle crashes.

- 599,000 students between the ages of 18 and 24 are unintentionally injured under the influence of alcohol.

- More than 696,000 students between the ages of 18 and 24 are assaulted by another student who has been drinking.

- More than 97,000 students between the ages of 18 and 24 are victims of alcohol-related sexual assault or date rape.

As IACLEA has predicted, adding accessibility to guns and other weapons to this mix is likely to lead to additional incidents of self-injury, accidental shootings, and homicides.

Our collective goal should be to make our college and university campuses as safe as possible. Allowing guns and other weapons on campus will not advance that goal; indeed, it will have the opposite effect and lead to additional deaths and injuries. The best way to keep our campuses safe is to retain colleges and universities on the list of places where individuals may not bring firearms.

10

Gun Crimes Cause Serious Harm to Children

Children's Defense Fund

The Children's Defense Fund, an American child advocacy and research group, works to protect every child's right to become a healthy and productive adult.

Too many children in the United States are affected by gun violence in the form of death, non-fatal gun injuries, or the emotional aftereffects. Recharged federal and state legislative action to strengthen gun control and gun safety laws would certainly help reduce youth gun violence, but individuals, families, and communities must also unite against the glamour of guns and offer positive alternatives toward purposeful and honorable activities.

After almost two decades of reporting on youth gun violence, CDF's [Children's Defense Fund] latest installment of *Protect Children, Not Guns* makes clear that our national obsession with guns continues to result in the senseless and unnecessary loss of young lives. The Centers for Disease Control and Prevention (CDC) reports that a total of 3,042 children and teens died by gunfire in 2007—a number nearly equal to the total number of U.S. combat deaths in Iraq and four times the number of American combat fatalities in Afghanistan to date [2010]. Another 17,523 children and teens suffered non-fatal gun injuries in 2007 and the emotional aftermath that follows. In each case it was a gun that ended or changed a young life forever.

Too Many Guns, Not Enough Gun Control

With over 280 million guns in civilian hands, the terrible truth is that there is no place to hide from gun violence. Children and teens are not safe from gun violence at school, at home, or anywhere else in America. A recent study found that rural and urban children and teens are equally likely to die from firearm injuries. Young people in urban areas are more likely to be homicide victims while rural children and teens are more likely to be victims of suicide or accidental shootings. The CDC estimates that nearly two million children live in homes with loaded and unlocked guns.

The epidemic of gun violence is particularly acute among young black men. In 2007, for the first time, more black than white children and teens were killed by gun violence. Black males 15 to 19 are more than five times as likely as white males of the same age and more than twice as likely as Hispanic males to be killed by firearms. They also are at substantially greater risk of being injured by gun violence than their white and Hispanic peers. Although their physical injuries heal, the emotional scars typically go untreated, leaving thousands of young survivors of gun violence in a hazy fog of trauma similar to that of soldiers returning from combat.

Among children and teens, firearm deaths are more likely to be homicides.

What will it take for us to stop this senseless loss of young lives? Common sense gun laws can make a difference. States with higher rates of gun ownership and weak gun control laws have the highest rates of firearm deaths of people of all ages. Although polls show that the majority of Americans favor common sense gun control laws that would stem the tide of gun violence, federal and state legislative reform has been difficult to achieve. We need political leaders who will protect our children by enacting legislation to limit the number of guns in our communities, control who can obtain firearms, and ensure that guns in the home are stored safely and securely.

But the responsibility to keep our children safe does not end here. Individuals and families must remove guns from their homes, mobilize community support to protect children from gun violence, stress nonviolent values and conflict resolution, refuse to buy or use products for children and teens that glamorize violence, and provide children and teens positive alternatives to the streets where they can feel safe and protected.

We must act to end the culture of violence that desensitizes us—young and old—to the value of life. We cannot allow these shots to go unheard. Our children and our society deserve more.

- Gunfire deaths among children and teens declined by nearly five percent between 2006 and 2007: 142 fewer children and teens died from firearms in 2007 than 2006. This includes 64 fewer homicides, 80 fewer suicides, and 16 fewer accidental firearm deaths. Deaths classified as "unknown" increased by 18 between 2006 and 2007.

- The number of children and teens killed by guns in 2007 would fill more than 122 public school classrooms of 25 students each. The number of preschoolers killed by firearms in 2007 (85) surpassed the number of law enforcement officers killed in the line of duty (57).

- Among children and teens, firearm deaths are more likely to be homicides. More than 70 percent of the firearm deaths of children and teens in 2007 were homicides; 22 percent were suicides. Among adults the trend is the exact opposite: 60 percent of firearm deaths of adults in 2007 were suicides while 38 percent were homicides.

• Ninety-five percent of firearm deaths of young people occurred among children and teens 10 to 19 years old. In fact, more 10- to 19-year-olds die from gunshot wounds than from any other cause except motor vehicle accidents.

• Children and teens killed by firearms are more likely to be boys (90 percent). Boys ages 15 to 19 are almost 10 times as likely as girls that age to commit suicide with a firearm. . . .

Common Sense Gun Safety Measures

Stronger federal legislation could help protect more children from the all too often fatal effects of gun violence. Measures that would help include:

Require consumer safety standards and childproof safety features for all firearms. All guns in this country should be childproof. One-third of all households with children have at least one firearm in the home. It is estimated that nearly two million children live in homes with an unlocked and loaded firearm. Federal law is silent on gun related consumer safety standards and child access prevention laws. In fact, the production and manufacture of firearms is exempt from oversight by the Consumer Product Safety Commission. As a result, many handguns do not contain easily-installed life-saving safety features. Only 27 states and the District of Columbia have attempted to keep children from accessing guns by passing child access prevention laws. Congress must pass legislation that subjects firearms to the same consumer product safety regulations that cover virtually all other consumer products. Congress must also require childproof safety features on all guns.

Close the gun show loophole. The Brady Handgun Violence Prevention Act requires federally licensed firearms dealers to conduct background checks on every sale. However, a loophole in the law allows private dealers to sell firearms without a license and avoid the required background checks. This loophole accounts for a large share of all gun sales, especially at gun shows. It is estimated that over 40 percent of all firearms in this country are sold by unlicensed sellers to buyers who did not have to submit to a background check. Eighteen states have attempted to block the loophole by requiring background checks for some categories of gun sales not covered by the Brady Law. Congress must pass legislation that closes the gun show loophole by requiring criminal background checks on anyone who attempts to purchase a gun.

Nearly two million children live in homes with loaded, unlocked guns.

Impose tougher restrictions on people convicted of a violent misdemeanor or a violent act as a juvenile. A related loophole exists for people adjuducated for violent and other serious offenses as juveniles who remain able to purchase guns as adults despite their past violent offenses. Under current law, a conviction for a violent misdemeanor does not prohibit a person from purchasing or possessing a gun. A study found that a person convicted of a violent misdemeanor was eight times more likely to be charged with a subsequent firearm and/or violent crime and one in three people convicted of a violent misdemeanor who tried to buy a handgun was arrested for a new crime within three years of acquiring the gun. Congress must pass legislation to block these loopholes and prohibit gun possession by individuals who have been convicted of certain violent misdemeanors and individuals who have been found delinquent for an act that would have been a felony if committed by an adult. . . .

A Place to Start: Gun-Free Homes

The Centers for Disease Control and Prevention estimates nearly two million children live in homes with loaded, unlocked guns. The presence of guns increases the risk of homicide and suicide. Parents often think they have adequately protected their children by safely storing their guns, but this sense of security seems misplaced. A study by the Harvard Injury Control Research Center found that 39 percent of children interviewed knew the location of their parents' firearms and 22 percent said they had handled the guns despite their parents' assertions to the contrary. Children under 10 were just as likely to have reported knowing where the guns were kept and having handled them as older children. Research shows that it is not enough to talk to children about the dangers of guns. Children exposed to gun safety programs are no less likely to play with guns than those who are not exposed to such classes. Removing guns from the home is one of the best ways to protect children and teens from gun deaths. . . .

Family violence in our society is epidemic, child abuse and neglect are widespread and children are exposed to television programming that glamorizes guns, violence and brutality. Conflict resolution skills are essential in this environment and not something that are typically taught in school or at home. Concerned parents can partner with schools, community groups and faith congregations to organize nonviolent conflict resolution support groups and push for adoption of a conflict resolution curriculum in your local school. . . .

Rejecting the Gun Culture

Adults and young people impacted by gun violence and concerned community members can unite to educate others about our crisis of gun violence. There are moving examples of parents and other family members of a child killed or injured by a gun channeling their grief and anger into broadening public understanding of the devastation of guns and increasing political support for stronger gun laws. Mobilize support to protect children from gun violence. . . .

Many children and teens, particularly in urban areas, are exposed to gangs, drugs, violence and guns on a daily basis.

We must offer positive alternatives and role models for children and teens, especially during after-school hours, weekends and summers. We must open our congregational, school and community doors and engage young people in purposeful activities. . . .

Our culture frequently glamorizes guns and violence in movies, television, music and on the internet. Many shows targeted at children have violent themes and language. Protest and refuse to buy or use products that glamorize or make violence socially acceptable or fun. Turn off violent programming and read or play with your children instead. Talk to them about the importance of rejecting violence as a cultural or personal value.

11

The Media Disregards Crimes Prevented by Defensive Gun Use

John R. Lott, Jr.

John R. Lott, Jr. is an academic and political commentator well known for his arguments against restrictions on owning and carrying guns. Lott has published many articles in academic journals and is the author of several books, including The Bias Against Guns *and* Freedomnomics.

For years citizens with permits to carry concealed handguns have used their weapons to prevent many crimes—robberies, rapes, even murders. Yet such heroic events are rarely covered by the media. And on the rare occasion in which such a story is reported, it is usually because the attacker was killed, or at least seriously wounded. This under-reporting of crime prevention and over-reporting of gun deaths have distorted the public's view of gun ownership and undermined the value of people being able to defend themselves and others.

The noise came suddenly from behind early Tuesday—feet rapidly pounding the pavement, voices cursing. Before Jim Shaver could turn around, he was knocked to the ground at East 13th Avenue and Mill Street, fighting off punches from two young men. Police said the assailants figured they'd found a drug dealer to rob, someone who'd have both drugs and money. They couldn't have been more wrong. Their victim was a 49-year-old nurse on his way to work—a nurse with a concealed weapons permit. The fists kept flying, even as Shaver told them—twice, he said—that he had a gun. Fearing for his life, Shaver pulled a .22-caliber revolver out of his coat pocket and fired several shots. One of them hit 19-year-old Damien Alexander Long in the right hip. Long's alleged accomplice, Brandon Heath Durrett, 20, wasn't injured. The pair ran off.

A man who police said kidnapped a 2-year-old child and robbed a disabled elderly woman of a medical monitor was in jail Friday after he was captured and held at gun point by a man with a license to carry a concealed handgun. . . . "I have never pulled a gun on anyone before, and I wouldn't have pulled a gun on this man if he had not run off with that little girl," [the man who stopped the crime] said. "That mother was screaming for her child. She was quite upset."

Awe-struck Phoenix police declared Mr. Vertigan a hero 'and gave him $500 and a new pistol for catching a cop killer after running out of ammunition in a gunfight with three heavily armed men. Mr. Vertigan . . . came upon three armed Mexican drug-traffickers fatally ambushing a uniformed Phoenix policeman who was patrolling alone in Phoenix's tough Maryvale precinct. Firing 14 shots with his left hand during a slam-and-bump car chase that left the killers' license number imprinted on the front of his own car, Mr. Vertigan emptied his Glock 31.357 Sig. He wounded the shooter, who was firing at him, and forced the getaway car to crash, slowing the shooter's partners long enough for pursuing police to seize them, as well as a pound of cocaine "eight balls" they were dealing from their white Lincoln. "I always felt that if my life was in danger or anyone around me was in immediate danger I never would hesitate to use that gun. Unfortunately, that day came," Mr. Vertigan said.

A man who tried to commit an armed robbery at a Bensalem convenience store Friday morning was thwarted by a customer who pulled out his own gun and fired five shots at the

crook. . . . Fearing he would be killed, police said, the customer began shooting at the suspect. . . . Police said the clerks
were "a little shaken up" after the attempted robbery—but
they guessed that the would-be robber was probably just as
shocked. "I'll bet he never expected that to happen," said Fred
Harran, Bensalem's deputy director of public safety.

Bad Events That Never Happened

All these recent cases involved individuals with permitted concealed handguns. During 1999 concealed permit holders have
prevented bank robberies, stopped what could have been a
bloody attack by gang members at a teenage girl's high school
graduation party, and stopped carjackings. In the couple of
months during which I was updating this book, armed citizens have helped capture murderers who had escaped prison;
stopped hostage taking at a business, a situation that otherwise surely would have resulted in multiple deaths; and prevented robberies and rapes. Residential attacks that were
stopped by citizens with guns during 1999 were extremely
common.

---

*Newsworthy bad events give people a warped impression
of the costs and benefits from having guns around.*

One of the bigger puzzles to me has been the news coverage on guns. Admittedly, some of it is easy to explain. Suppose
a media outlet has two stories to choose from: one in which
there is a dead body on the ground and it is a sympathetic
person like a victim, another in which a woman brandishes a
gun and the attacker runs away, no shots are fired, no dead
bodies are on the ground, and no crime is actually consum-
mated. It seems pretty obvious which story is going to get the
news coverage. Yet if we really want to answer the question of
which policies will save lives, we must take into consideration
not only the newsworthy bad events but also the bad events

that never happen because people are able to defend themselves. Unfortunately, the newsworthy bad events give people a warped impression of the costs and benefits from having guns around.

Even when defensive gun uses are mentioned in the press, those mentions do not focus on typical defensive gun uses. The news stories focus primarily on the extremely rare cases in which the attacker is killed, though a few times press stories do mention cases of a gun being used to seriously wound an attacker. News coverage of defensive gun uses in which a would-be victim simply brandished a gun are essentially unheard-of. I don't think one has to rely on a conspiracy explanation to understand why this type of news coverage occurs, for it is not that surprising that dead attackers are considered more newsworthy than prevented attacks in which nobody was harmed. Even so, it is still important to recognize how this coverage can color people's perspective on how guns are used defensively. Since most people probably are very reticent to take a life, if they believe that defensive gun use almost always results in the death of an attacker, they will become more uncomfortable with guns. . . .

Prevented Mass Shootings Are Not Newsworthy

Another puzzle is the lack of coverage given to cases in which citizens with guns have prevented multiple-victim public shootings from occurring. Given the intense concern generated by these attacks, one would think that people would be interested in knowing how these attacks were stopped.

For a simple comparison, take the justified news coverage accorded the heroic actions of Dave Sanders, the Columbine High School teacher who helped protect some of the students and was killed in the process [April 1999]. By the Sunday morning five days after the incident, a Lexis-Nexis search (a type of on-line computer search that includes news media databases) indicates that over 250 of the slightly over 1,000 news stories around the country on this tragedy had mentioned this hero.

Contrast this with other school attacks in which the crimes were stopped well before the police were able to arrive. Take, for example, the October 1997 shooting spree at a high school in Pearl, Mississippi, . . . which left two students dead. It was stopped by Joel Myrick, an assistant principal. He retrieved his permitted concealed handgun from his car and physically immobilized the shooter for about five minutes before police arrived.

A Lexis-Nexis search indicates that 687 articles appeared in the first month after the attack. Only 19 stories mentioned Myrick in any way. Only a little more than half of these mentioned he used a gun to stop the attack. Some stories simply stated Myrick was "credited by police with helping capture the boy" or that "Myrick disarmed the shooter." A later story reported by Dan Rather on CBS noted that "Myrick eventually subdued the young gunman." Such stories provide no explanation of how Myrick accomplished this feat.

The school-related shooting in Edinboro, Pennsylvania [April 1998], which left one teacher dead, was stopped only after James Strand, the owner of a nearby restaurant, pointed a shotgun at the shooter when he was finishing reloading his gun. The police did not arrive until eleven minutes later. At least 596 news stories discussed this crime during the next month, yet only 35 mentioned Strand. Once again, the media ignored that a gun was used to stop the crime. The *New York Daily News* explained that Strand "persuaded [the killer] to surrender," while the *Atlanta Journal* wrote how he "chased [the killer] down and held him until police came." Saying that Strand "persuaded" the attacker makes it sound as if Strand were simply an effective speaker.

Neither Myrick nor Strand was killed during their heroics. That might explain why they were ignored to a greater degree than Dave Sanders in the Columbine attack. Yet one suspects a more politically correct explanation—especially when the media generally ignore defensive gun use. With five public-school-related shootings occurring during the 1997–1998 school year, one might have thought that the fact that two of them were stopped by guns would register in the public debate over such shootings.

Bad events that never occur are not nearly as news-worthy as actual bad events.

The media bias can be amply illustrated by other examples as well. Take the example of the July [1999] attack in Atlanta, which left nine people dead. Mark Barton killed people working at two stock brokerages. It did deserve the extensive news coverage that it received. Yet, within the next week and a half, there were three cases around Atlanta in which citizens with guns stopped similar attacks from occurring, and these incidents were given virtually no news coverage. They were an attack at a Lavonia, Georgia, store by a fired worker; an attack by a mental patient at an Atlanta hospital; and an Atlanta truckjacking. The last two incidents were stopped by citizens with permitted concealed handguns. The first was stopped by someone who had only been allowed to buy a gun hours before the attack because of Georgia's instant background check system. Meanwhile, a week after the Atlanta massacre, another attack, which left three people dead at a business in Birmingham, Alabama, again generated national television news coverage on all the networks and was the lead story on the CBS and NBC evening news.

The Media's Bias for Gun Attacks

Again, I can see that bad events that never occur are not nearly as newsworthy as actual bad events. Yet multiple-victim attacks using methods other than guns are frequently ignored.

On May 3, 1999, Steve Abrams drove his Cadillac into a crowded preschool playground because he "wanted to execute innocent children." Two children died horrible deaths as one was mangled under the wheels and the other pinned to a tree by the car, and another five were badly injured. One woman's son was so badly mauled that "teachers and other parents stepped between [her] and the Cadillac to prevent her from seeing her son's battered body" even though he was still alive. Yet only one television network provided even a passing reference to this attack. One very obvious news angle, it seems to me, would be to link this attack to the various public school attacks. Compare this news coverage with the attention generated by Buford Furrow's August 10, 1999, assault on a Jewish community center, which left five people wounded, three of them young boys. Multiple-victim knife attacks have been ignored by the national media, and few people would realize that there were 1,884 bombing incidents in the United States in 1996, which left a total of 34 people dead and 365 people injured.

The Gun Control Question

The news coverage is also constantly framed as, "Is more gun control the answer?" The question is never asked, "Have increased regulations encouraged these attacks by making potential victims more vulnerable? Do these attacks demonstrate the importance of letting people be able to defend themselves?" . . .

Yet without academic evidence that existing regulations such as gun-free zones, the Brady law, and gun locks produce desirable results, it is surprising that in 2000 we are now debating what new gun-control laws to pass. With that in mind, 294 academics from institutions as diverse as Harvard, Stanford, Northwestern, the University of Pennsylvania, and UCLA released an open letter to Congress during 1999 stating that the proposed new gun laws are "ill advised." They wrote that

"With the 20,000 gun laws already on the books, we advise Congress, before enacting yet more new laws, to investigate whether many of the existing laws may have contributed to the problems we currently face."

An effective as well as moving piece I recently read was written by Dale Anema, a father whose son was trapped for hours inside the Columbine High School building during the April 1999 attack. His agony while waiting to hear what happened to his son touches any parent's worst fears. Because he had witnessed this tragedy, he described his disbelief over the policy debate:

> Two pending gun bills are immediately dropped by the Colorado legislature. One is a proposal to make it easier for law-abiding citizens to carry concealed weapons; the other is a measure to prohibit municipalities from suing gun manufacturers. I wonder: If two crazy hoodlums can walk into a "gun-free" zone full of our kids, and police are totally incapable of defending the children, why would anyone want to make it harder for law-abiding adults to defend themselves and others? . . . Of course, nobody on TV mentions that perhaps gun-free zones are potential magnets to crazed killers.

12

US Gun Laws Fuel Mexican Drug Wars

Juliet A. Leftwich

Juliet A. Leftwich is the legal director of Legal Community Against Violence, a national public interest law center dedicated to preventing gun violence.

The increasingly violent bloodshed in Mexico caused by the Mexican drug cartels is a direct result of the weak gun-control laws in the United States. Because gun sales in Mexico are strictly regulated, drug lords are turning to US gun dealers, who easily and legally sell them guns. The US Congress needs to stand up against the powerful gun lobby and enact federal legislation to strengthen its gun laws, such as requiring background checks for every gun purchase and banning assault weapons.

Anyone who needs convincing that our nation's gun laws are dangerously inadequate should consider the devastating impact those laws are having on our neighbor to the south, Mexico. Firearm-related violence across the border has skyrocketed recently in bloody battles between Mexican drug cartels and Mexican authorities, resulting in the slaughter of police officers, soldiers, judges, prosecutors, reporters and innocent bystanders. Because Mexico's strict gun laws make it extremely difficult for civilians to purchase firearms, the increasing gun violence raises an obvious question: Where are the drug cartels buying their guns? Unfortunately, they're buying them right here in the United States.

The Flow of Illegal Guns

According to a report issued by the U.S. State Department on Feb. 27 [2009], more than 5,000 people were killed in the Mexican drug wars in 2008. The report states that Mexican authorities seized nearly 40,000 illegal firearms in 2008 and that 95 percent of the guns traced were purchased in the United States. Not surprisingly, the escalating violence has begun to spill over into this country.

The reason Mexican drug lords look to America for their guns is clear: In most states they can easily buy guns, including assault weapons and .50-caliber rifles, from private sellers without a background check, no questions asked.

Undocumented sales by unlicensed persons . . . account for an estimated 40 percent of all gun sales.

Gun sales in Mexico, in contrast, are strictly regulated, as they are in other industrialized nations outside of the United States. The reason shady gun dealers and private sellers here are willing to supply the illegal Mexican market is also clear: It is a highly lucrative business and our gun laws make it unlikely that they will ever get caught.

Three changes to our federal firearms laws would help dramatically stem the flow of illegal guns, both in Mexico and here at home.

Necessary Changes to Gun Laws

The first would be to close the "private sale loophole," which allows unlicensed persons to sell guns without conducting a background check on the purchaser. Under existing federal law, background check and other record-keeping requirements are only imposed upon licensed firearms dealers. However, undocumented sales by unlicensed persons—which can legally occur at gun shows or any other location—account for an estimated 40 percent of all gun sales. Because of this massive loophole, criminals and other prohibited persons can easily buy guns throughout most of the United States (only California and Rhode Island require background checks on all gun purchasers). It should surprise no one, therefore, that Mexican drug gangs have seized upon this loophole to funnel guns into Mexico.

The bloodshed in Mexico and America could also be curtailed if Congress banned assault weapons and .50-caliber rifles (rifles used by armed forces worldwide that combine long range, accuracy and massive power). Congress enacted an assault weapon ban in 1994, but allowed that law to expire in 2004. Now only seven states, including California, ban assault weapons, and California is the only state to ban .50-caliber rifles.

As a result of this regulatory vacuum, assault weapons and .50-caliber rifles are proliferating on the domestic market. They are also being purchased in the United States and smuggled across the border for use by the drug cartels, ever eager to increase their firepower over Mexican authorities. During a recent press conference in Phoenix focused on combating drug cartels in Mexico, Attorney General Eric Holder linked the proliferation of military-style weapons to the violence along the Mexican border, noting that a federal assault weapon ban would have a positive impact.

Finally, Congress could significantly reduce gun violence, both domestically and in Mexico, if it strengthened regulation and oversight of firearms dealers by repealing the so-called Tiahrt Amendments, annual riders to the U.S. Department of Justice's appropriations bill which significantly hinder law enforcement's ability to prosecute corrupt dealers and other criminals.

Prosecute Dealers Who Traffic Guns

According to the Bureau of Alcohol, Tobacco, Firearms and Explosives, firearms dealers are a major source of trafficked firearms here and in Mexico. Trafficked guns are frequently sold by a dealer to a "straw purchaser," a person with a clean criminal record who purchases a gun on behalf of a convicted felon or other prohibited person, often in a manner that would be obvious to any dealer who is paying attention. Business is booming for dealers who have set up shop along the 2,000-mile U.S.-Mexican border, where more than 6,600 dealers now sell their wares.

Weak gun laws are directly contributing to the senseless bloodshed in Mexico and at home.

Law enforcement efforts to prosecute dealers engaged in gun trafficking are significantly hampered by the Tiahrt Amendments, which: 1) prohibit ATF from releasing gun trace data, used to determine where a crime gun was purchased and historically shared by law enforcement agencies to detect patterns of criminal behavior; 2) require the destruction of approved gun purchaser records within 24 hours (records of handgun purchases in California, in contrast, are never destroyed, facilitating efficient crime gun tracing); and 3) prohibit ATF from requiring gun dealers to submit inventories, allowing unscrupulous dealers to claim that they simply "lost" guns that are later recovered in crime. These amendments, added to appropriations bills since 2003 at the behest of the gun lobby, have tied the hands of law enforcement seeking to prosecute gun dealers who supply the illegal market.

Public opinion polls consistently show overwhelming support for common-sense reforms to our nation's gun laws. According to three of those polls, 92 percent of respondents favor mandatory criminal background checks for all gun purchasers; 65 percent favor banning assault weapons; 90 percent believe police should be allowed to share information about purchasers and sellers of crime guns; and 86 percent favor requiring dealers to conduct annual inventories.

Although President [Barack] Obama has also expressed support for strengthening background checks, banning assault weapons and repealing the Tiahrt trace data restrictions, his fellow Democrats have shown little appetite for a fight with the National Rifle Association, despite the fact that our nation's weak gun laws are directly contributing to the senseless bloodshed in Mexico and at home. How much longer are members of Congress going to ignore the will of the American people and continue their shameless pandering to the gun lobby? Probably for as long as we continue to let them.

13

Cultural Factors Play a Role in Gun Violence

Richard Florida

Richard Florida is senior editor at The Atlantic *magazine and director of the Martin Prosperity Institute, a think tank concerned with the underlying forces behind global economic prosperity. Florida is the author of the books* The Rise of the Creative Class *and* Who's Your City?

Psychological studies have shown that people living in southern and western regions of the United States tend to view violence as an appropriate response to insults or when they believe their honor or property has been attacked. This "culture of honor," as it has been termed, appears to be a significant factor in school violence, particularly among males who have experienced some form of bullying, humiliation, or rejection. It is even more worrisome that this culture of honor seems to be spreading into both urban and rural communities.

The mass shootings in Tucson over the weekend [January 8, 2011] led to all sorts of exercises in arm-chair psychology. The media was quick to portray the shooter Jared Lee Loughner as unhinged and paranoid, digging up his Internet ravings and probing former friends and classmates for detailed testimonials of his bizarre statements and aggressive behavior. And, following its polarization meme, we were subjected to endless accounts of how America's heated and "vitriolic" political climate helped to trigger such action.

But what can psychology tell us about the specific ways that regional, locational, and geographic factors can affect gun violence and mass shootings in particular?

I was surprised by what I found out when I asked my colleague Jason Rentfrow, the distinguished social psychologist at Cambridge University [United Kingdom], about this. While some continue to attribute gun violence and mass shootings to hot climates in the U.S. and elsewhere—"Living in a hot and uncomfortable climate makes people irritable and rates of violence go up," Rentfrow summarizes the—preponderance of studies focus on a "culture of honor" that is especially pervasive in Southern and Western states. This is something that pundits and commentators need to take a good deal more seriously because, if it is correct, and a considerable body of research suggests that it is, it suggests that deep-seated regional and cultural factors play a substantial role in mass violence.

Examining the "Culture of Honor"

The classic study of the subject is by Richard Nisbett, a social psychologist at the University of Michigan. In his paper "Violence and Regional Culture," published in the *American Psychologist* in 1993, Nisbett examined the higher rate of violence in the U.S. south, which he notes has been established since the time of revolution. After considering possible explanations having to do with poverty, slavery, and even the region's hotter climate, he found a different answer in a cultural vestige of pastoralism: a deep "culture of honor" in which residents place an extraordinary value on personal reputation, family, and property. Threats to these things provoke aggressive reactions, leading to higher rates of murder and domestic violence. Here is how Nisbett himself explains it:

> Southerners do not endorse violence in the abstract more than do Northerners, nor do they endorse violence in all specific forms of circumstances. Rather, they are more likely to endorse violence as an appropriate response to insults, as

a means of self protection, and as a socialization tool in training children. This is the characteristic cultural pattern of herding societies the world over. Consistent with the culture-of-honor interpretation, it is argument-related and not felony-related homicide that is more common in the South . . .

There is another sense in which the culture of honor might turn out to be self-sustaining or even capable of expanding into mainstream culture. The culture is a variant of warrior culture the world over, and its independent invention count-less times, combined with the regularities in its themes having to do with glorification of masculine attributes, suggests that it may be a particularly alluring stance that may be capable of becoming functionally autonomous. Many observers have noted that contemporary Southern backcountry culture, including music, dress, and social stance, is spreading beyond its original geographical confines and becoming a part of the fabric of rural, and even urban, working-class America.

Perhaps for the young males who adopt it, this culture provides a romantic veneer to everyday existence. If so, it is distinctly possible that the violence characteristic of this culture is also spreading beyond its confines. An understanding of the culture and its darker side would thus remain important for the foreseeable future.

The culture of honor . . . sees violence as an "appropriate response to insults" and as "a means of self-protection."

Culture of Honor and School Violence

Rentfrow also pointed me to a more recent study by Ryan P. Brown, Lindsey Osterman, and Collin Barnes of the University of Oklahoma, published in *Psychological Science* in 2009, which reinforces Nisbett's findings and suggests that the culture of honor plays a particularly significant role in high school violence. The study found the culture of honor to be significantly associated with two indices of school violence: the percentage of high school students who reported having brought a weapon to school during the past month; and the prevalence of actual school shootings over a 20-year period. The authors summarize their key findings this way:

Some researchers have suggested that the apparent relationship between general acts of violence and the culture of honor in the United States might be at least partially explained by demographic differences between Southern and Western states, on the one hand, and Northern and Eastern states, on the other, rather than being a product of cultural differences. Indeed, culture-of-honor states are typically hotter, more rural, and poorer than non-culture-of-honor states, and any of these differences might explain the link between culture of honor and violence.

However, the state-level demographic variables that we examined—which included temperature, rurality, social composition, and indices of economic and social insecurity—were unable to account for the association between culture of honor and our school-violence indicators, and also were inconsistent predictors of the school-violence variables across the two studies. This marks an important difference between these indicators of school violence and more general indicators of violent crime among adults, which typically show stronger and more consistent associations with temperature, rurality, and environmental-insecurity measures similar to the ones we used.

This difference suggests that school violence is a somewhat distinct form of aggression that should not be viewed through standard lenses. That the culture of honor appears to be such a robust predictor of school violence supports the hypothesis that school violence might be partially a product of long-term or recent experiences of social marginalization, humiliation, rejection, or bullying, all of which represent honor threats with special significance to people (particularly males) living in culture-of-honor states.

I am amazed how well this explanation seems to fit the emerging facts and context of the mass violence in Tucson. I don't mean the obvious fact that the shooting happened in a Sunbelt city—Tucson is a sophisticated college town, not the sort of rural backwater Nisbett had in mind. It is the nature of the culture of honor itself and the way it acts on and through marginalized young males, just like Loughner. The culture of honor, as Nisbett describes it, sees violence as an "appropriate response to insults" and as "a means of self-protection."

Numerous media reports note that Loughner grew more obsessed with Congresswoman [Gabrielle] Giffords after he felt she did not give him a respectful answer to the question he asked her at an earlier forum. Then there are the results of the University of Oklahoma study which finds the culture of honor to be a particularly robust predictor of high school violence, especially among young males who have been marginalized, bullied, rejected, or faced other "honor threats." And, Nisbett's some two-decades-old warning that the culture of honor is not something that is necessarily geographically bounded but seems to spreading into broader aspects of young male working-class enclaves in both urban and rural communities is as prescient as it is chilling.

Organizations to Contact

The editors have compiled the following list of organizations concerned with the issues debated in this book. The descriptions are derived from materials provided by the organizations. All have publications or information available for interested readers. The list was compiled on the date of publication of the present volume; names; addresses, phone and fax numbers, and e-mail and Internet addresses may change. Be aware that many organizations take several weeks or longer to respond to inquiries, so allow as much time as possible.

American Civil Liberties Union (ACLU)
125 Broad St., 18th Fl., New York, NY   10004
(212) 549-2500
website: www.aclu.org

The ACLU champions the rights set forth in the US Constitution. The union interprets the Second Amendment as a guarantee to form militias, not as a guarantee of the individual right to own and bear firearms and believes that gun control is constitutional and necessary. The ACLU publishes the Blog of Rights in addition to policy statements and reports, many of which are available on its website.

Brady Campaign to Prevent Gun Violence
1225 Eye St. NW, Ste. 1100, Washington, DC   20005
(202) 898-0793
website: www.bradycampaign.org

Established by former White House press secretary and gun violence victim James Brady and his wife, Sarah, the Brady Campaign's primary goal is to create an America free from gun violence. Through grassroots activism, the organization works to reform the gun industry, educate the public about gun violence, and develop sensible regulations to reduce gun violence. The organization publishes a blog, fact sheets, issue briefs, and special reports on its website, including "Guns and Hate: A Lethal Combination."

Cato Institute
1000 Massachusetts Ave. NW, Washington, DC   20001-5403
(202) 842-0200 • fax: (202) 842-3490
website: www.cato.org

The Cato Institute is a libertarian public-policy research foundation. It evaluates government policies and offers reform proposals and commentary on its website. Its publications include the blog "Cato@Liberty," the magazine *Regulation*, the *Cato Policy Report*, and books such as *Rehabilitating Lochner: Defending Individual Rights Against Progressive Reform*.

Citizens Committee for the Right to Keep and Bear Arms (CCRKBA)
12500 NE Tenth Pl., Bellevue, WA   98005
(425) 454-4911 • fax: (425) 451-3959
e-mail: AdminForWeb@ccrkba.org
website: www.ccrkba.org

The committee believes that the US Constitution's Second Amendment guarantees and protects the right of individual Americans to own guns. The organization works to educate the public concerning this right and to lobby legislators to prevent the passage of gun-control laws. The committee is affiliated with the Second Amendment Foundation and has more than six hundred thousand members. It publishes several magazines, including *Gun Week* and *Women & Guns*. News releases, fact sheets, and editorials are also available on its website.

Coalition for Gun Control
1488 Queen St. West, Toronto, ON
  M6K 3K3
(416) 604-0209
e-mail: 71417.763@compuserve.com
website: www.guncontrol.ca

The coalition was founded in the wake of the Montreal massacre in which a man with a Ruger Mini-14 and large-capacity magazine shot twenty-eight people at l'Ecole Polytechnique, killing fourteen young female engineering students. The Canadian organization was formed to reduce gun death, injury, and crime. It supports strict safe gun storage requirements, possession permits, a complete ban on assault weapons, and tougher restrictions on handguns. The coalition publishes press releases and backgrounders. Its website provides information on firearms deaths and injuries, illegal gun trafficking, and Canada's gun-control law.

Coalition to Stop Gun Violence (CSGV)
1424 L St. NW, Ste. 2-1, Washington, DC   20005
(202) 408-0061
e-mail: csgv@csgv.org
website: www.csgv.org

The CSGV was founded in 1975 and is composed of 48 civic, professional, and religious organizations working to reduce gun violence. Its mission is to stop gun violence by fostering effective community and national action. The organization lobbies at the local, state, and federal levels to ban the sale of handguns to individuals and to institute licensing and registration of all firearms. Its publications include various informational sheets on gun violence, press releases, and fact sheets. On its website, CSGV publishes blogs and articles on assault weapons, gun laws, and other gun-violence issues.

Gun Owners of America (GOA)
8001 Forbes Pl., Ste. 102, Springfield, VA   22151
(703) 321-8585 • fax: (703) 321-8408
website: http://gunowners.org

GOA is a nonprofit lobbying organization that defends the Second Amendment rights of gun owners. It has developed a network of attorneys to help fight court battles to protect gun owners' rights. GOA also works with members of Congress, state legislators, and local citizens to protect gun ranges and local gun clubs from closure by the government. On its website the organization publishes fact sheets; articles directed towards women, such as "Women, Stop Watching Oprah and

Learn to Love Guns;" various informational articles, including "Does the Media Suppress Self-Defense?" and links to op-ed articles, including "Righting 'wrongs' based on wrong interpretations of 'rights.'"

Independence Institute
13952 Denver West Pkwy., Ste. 400, Golden, CO   80401
(303) 279-6536 • fax: (303) 279-4176
e-mail: kay@i2i.org
website: www.i2i.org

The institute is a non-partisan, non-profit public policy research organization that supports gun ownership as both a civil liberty and a constitutional right. Its website contains blogs, articles, fact sheets, and commentary from a variety of sources and includes the Second Amendment Project, which provides perspective on topics ranging from legal reform to gun rights.

Jews for the Preservation of Firearms Ownership (JPFO)
PO Box 270143, Hartford, WI   53027
(262) 673-9745 • fax: (262) 673-9746
e-mail: jpfo@jpfo.org
website: www.jpfo.org

JPFO is a non-profit educational civil rights organization that believes Jewish law mandates self-defense. Its primary goal is the elimination of the idea that gun control is a socially useful public policy in any country. On its website JPFO provides links to firearms commentary.

Legal Community Against Violence (LCAV)
268 Bush St., #555, San Francisco, CA   94104
(415) 433-2062 • fax: (415) 433-3357
website: www.lcav.org

The Legal Community Against Violence is a public interest law center dedicated to preventing gun violence. Founded by lawyers, LCAV is devoted to providing legal assistance in support of gun violence prevention. LCAV publishes *Reports and Analysis*, including "Guns in Public Places: The Increasing Threat of Hidden Guns in America," and "Open Carrying: Provocative Conduct, Dangerous Consequences," as well as op eds and links to letters to the editor that provide legal analysis and commentary on gun violence prevention issues.

National Crime Prevention Council (NCPC)

2001 Jefferson Davis Highway, Ste. 901, Arlington, VA   22202
(202) 466-6272
website: www.ncpc.org

The NCPC is a branch of the US Department of Justice. Through its programs and educational materials, the council works to teach Americans how to reduce crime and to address its causes. It provides readers with information on gun control and gun violence. The NCPC's publications include the monthly newsletter *Catalyst*, and articles, brochures, and fact sheets, many of which are available on its website.

National Rifle Association of America (NRA)

11250 Waples Mill Rd., Fairfax, VA   22030
(800) 672-3888
website: www.nra.org

With over four million members, the NRA is America's largest organization of gun owners. It is also the primary lobbying group for those who oppose gun-control laws. The NRA believes that such laws violate the US Constitution and do nothing to reduce crime. In addition to its monthly magazines *America's 1st Freedom, American Rifleman, American Hunter, NRA Insights*, and *Shooting Sports USA*, the NRA publishes numerous books, bibliographies, reports, and pamphlets on gun ownership, gun safety, and gun control, some of which are available on its website.

Second Amendment Foundation (SAF)

12500 NE Tenth Pl., Bellevue, WA   98005
(206) 454-7012 • fax: (206) 451-3959

e-mail: AdminForWeb@saf.org
website: www.saf.org

A sister organization to the Citizens Committee for the Right to Keep and Bear Arms, the foundation is dedicated to informing Americans about their Second Amendment right to keep and bear firearms. It believes that gun-control laws violate this right. The foundation publishes numerous books, including *Armed America, Armed: New Perspectives on Gun Control, CCW: Carrying Concealed Weapons*, and *The Concealed Handgun Manual: How to Choose, Carry, and Shoot a Gun in Self Defense*. "Gun Rights Frequently Asked Questions," as well as various reports, articles and commentary on gun issues are available on its website.

US Department of Justice (DOJ) Office of Justice Programs
810 Seventh St. NW, Washington, DC   20531
website: www.ojp.usdoj.gov

The Department of Justice strives to protect citizens by maintaining effective law enforcement, crime prevention, crime detection, and prosecution and rehabilitation of offenders. Through its Office of Justice Programs, the department operates the National Institute of Justice, the Office of Juvenile Justice and Delinquency Prevention, the Bureau of Justice Statistics, and the Office for Victims of Crime. The Bureau of Justice Statistics provides research on crime and criminal justice. The offices of the DOJ publish a variety of crime-related documents on their respective websites.

Violence Policy Center (VPC)
1730 Rhode Island Ave. NW, Ste. 1014
Washington, DC   20036
(202) 822-8200
website: www.vpc.org

The center is a nonprofit educational foundation that conducts research on firearms violence. It works to educate the public concerning the dangers of guns and supports gun-control measures. The center's publications include *Drive-By America, Accessories to Murder, A Shrinking Minority: The Continuing Decline of Gun Ownership in America,* and *When Men Murder Women: An Analysis of 2008 Homicide Data.* On the center's website are fact sheets, press releases, and studies on concealed-carry laws, assault weapons, and other firearm violence issues.

Bibliography

Books

Ben Agger — *There Is a Gunman on Campus: Tragedy and Terror at Virginia Tech.* Lanham, MD: Rowman & Littlefield, 2008.

Pjeter D. Baldridge, editor — *Gun Ownership and the Second Amendment.* Hauppauge, NY: Nova Science Publishers, 2009.

Chris Bird — *Thank God I Had a Gun: True Accounts of Self-Defense.* San Antonio, TX: Privateer Publications, 2006.

Joan Burbick — *Gun Show Nation: Gun Culture and American Democracy.* New York: New Press, 2006.

Brian Doherty — *Gun Control on Trial: Inside the Supreme Court Battle Over the Second Amendment.* Washington, DC: Cato Institute, 2008.

Richard Feldman — *Ricochet: Confessions of a Gun Lobbyist.* Hoboken, NJ: John Wiley & Sons, 2008.

Kristin A. Goss — *Disarmed: The Missing Movement for Gun Control in America.* Princeton, NJ: Princeton University Press, 2006.

Alan Gottlieb and Dave Workman — *America Fights Back: Armed Self-Defense in a Violent Age.* Bellevue, WA: Merril Press, 2007.

Alan Gottlieb and
Dave Workman

These Dogs Don't Hunt: The Democrats' War on Guns. Bellevue, WA: Merril Press, 2008.

Stephen P.
Halbrook

The Founders' Second Amendment: Origins of the Right to Bear Arms. Chicago: Ivan R. Dee, 2008.

Bernard E.
Harcourt

Language of the Gun: Youth, Crime, and Public Policy. Chicago: University of Chicago Press, 2006.

Dennis A.
Henigan

Lethal Logic: Exploding the Myths that Paralyze American Gun Policy. Washington, DC: Potomac Books, 2009.

Kathy Jackson

The Cornered Cat: A Woman's Guide to Concealed Carry. Hamilton, MI: White Feather Press, LLC, 2010.

David B. Kopel

Aiming for Liberty: The Past, Present, and Future of Freedom and Self Defense. Bellevue, WA: Merril Press, 2009.

Mark Pogrebin,
N. Prabha
Unnithan, Paul
Stretesky

Guns, Violence, and Criminal Behavior: The Offender's Perspective. Boulder, CO: Lynne Rienner Publishers, 2009.

John A. Rich

Wrong Place, Wrong Time: Trauma and Violence in the Lives of Young Black Men. Baltimore: Johns Hopkins University Press, 2009.

Lucinda Roy

No Right to Remain Silent: The Tragedy at Virginia Tech. Van Nuys, CA: Harmony, 2009.

Robert J. Spitzer   *The Politics of Gun Control*, 4th
Edition. Washington, DC: CQ Press,
2008.

Mark Walters and   *Lessons from Armed America.*
Kathy Jackson   Hamilton, MI: White Feather Press,
LLC, 2009.

Timothy Wheeler   *Keeping Your Family Safe: The*
and E. John   *Responsibilities of Firearm Ownership.*
Wipfler   Bellevue, WA: Merril Press, 2009.

Periodicals and Internet Sources

Ben Adler   "Conservatives Make Inaccurate
Arguments Against Gun Control,"
Newsweek, January 18, 2011.

Ellen S. Alberding   "Philanthropy Must Challenge the
Idea that Gun Violence Can't Be
Stopped," *The Chronicle of
Philanthropy*, January 14, 2011.

Frida Berrigan   "Too Many Guns," *Huffington Post*,
October 23, 2008. www.huffington
post.com.

Jimmy Carter   "What Happened to the Ban on
Assault Weapons?" *New York Times*,
April 26, 2009.

Steve Chapman   "The Unconcealed Truth about
Carrying Guns," *Reason*, March 31,
2011. www.reason.com.

Saul Cornell   "What the 'Right to Bear Arms'
Really Means," *Salon*, January 15,
2011. www.salon.com.

Diane Dimond	"Packing Heat at College," *Huffington Post*, March 1, 2011. www.huffington post.com.
John J. Donohue	"It Takes Laws to Control the Bad Guys," *New York Times*, January 12, 2011.
James Alan Fox	"More Guns Means More Guns," *New York Times*, January 12, 2011.
Morris Goodman	"Gun Violence in America Calls for Gun Control," *The News-Herald*, January 17, 2011.
Michael Grunwald	"Tucson Tragedy: Is Gun Control a Dead Issue?" *Time*, January 24, 2011.
Thomas L. Harnisch	"Concealed Weapons on State College Campuses: In Pursuit of Individual Liberty and Collective Security," American Association of State Colleges and Universities (AASCU), November 2008. www.aascu.org.
Bob Herbert	"How Many Deaths Are Enough?" *New York Times*, January 17, 2011.
Joshua E. Keating	"Armed, But Not Necessarily Dangerous," *Foreign Policy*, January 11, 2011. www.foreignpolicy.com.
Nicholas D. Kristof	"Why Not Regulate Guns as Seriously as Toys?" *New York Times*, January 12, 2011.

Juliet A. Leftwich   "Worse than Iraq: Guns Kill More
                     Americans at Home in Six Weeks
                     than in Four Years of War," *The
                     Recorder*, October 12, 2007.

W. Scott Lewis   "Empty Holsters on Campus," *The
                     Washington Times*, October 24, 2007.

Sylvia Longmire   "Guns in Mexico: A Challenge to
                     Obama and the NRA," *San Diego
                     Union-Tribune*, June 23, 2011.

John R. Lott, Jr.   "More Guns, Less Crime?: The Case
                     for Arming Yourself," *New York
                     Times*, January 12, 2011.

Michael Luo   "Mental Health and Guns: Do
                     Background Checks Do Enough?"
                     New York Times, April 19, 2007.

Heather Martens   "When Background Checks Are
                     Given a Chance, They Work,"
                     Minnesota Public Radio, March 23,
                     2011. www.minnesotapublicradio.org.

Roger Simon   "The Everyday Crisis of Gun
                     Violence," *Politico*, April 7, 2009.
                     www.politico.com.

Ron Smith   "Face the Facts: Gun Control Laws
                     Don't Save Lives," *The Baltimore Sun*,
                     January 20, 2011.

Robert J. Spitzer   "Campuses Just Say 'No' to Guns,"
                     Huffington Post, February 27, 2011.
                     www.huffingtonpost.com.

Daniel Stone "Is Gun Violence the Cost of Freedom?" *Newsweek*, January 13, 2011.

John Stossel "Guns Save Lives: Why the Right to Keep and Bear Arms Is Essential in a Free Society," *Reason*, June 24, 2010. www.reason.com.

Mike Stuckey "Record Numbers Licensed to Pack Heat," *MSNBC.com*, June 24, 2010. www.msnbc.msn.com.

Janalee Tobias "Columbine Was an Easy Target—Guns Protect Schools from Criminals," *US News & World Report*, April 20, 2009.

Index

A

Abrams, Steve, 90

Accessibility of guns
  to children, 16, 32, 78–79, 80, 82
  leads to crime, 17–22
  as protective, 14–15, 23–28

Accidents
  children, 20, 32, 77, 79
  concealed weapons, 72
  as exaggerated, 23, 40
  rural vs. urban, 78
  statistics/totals, 11, 18, 19–20, 30

Alcohol and guns, 62, 72, 76

American Association of State Colleges and Universities, 68–69

American history and myths, 13–14

Anema, Dale, 91

Appalachian School of Law shooting (2002), 70

Armed America (Cassidy), 12

Arms trafficking
  gun shows and illegal guns, 21, 47–48, 56–57, 93–94
  laws that enable, 94, 95, 96
  laws to prevent, 32, 37
  US guns and Mexican drug war, 92–96

Assassinations and attempts, 11, 50–51

Assault weapons
  availability, 43–49, 47, 93, 94

gun control/ban support, 9, 31, 35, 92, 94, 95
  legality, 30–31

ATF. *See* Bureau of Alcohol, Tobacco, and Firearms (ATF)

Attorney General, reporting, 54

Australia, 41

B

Background checks
  Brady Act, 30, 32, 47, 48, 50–51, 80
  current system is ineffective in preventing violence, 43–49
  instant, Georgia, 89
  loopholes and secondary sales, 21, 30–31, 32, 43, 46–49, 51–52, 55–57, 80–81, 92, 93–94
  political support, 12–13, 34, 96
  public support, 9, 35, 95
  updated system will help prevent gun violence, 50–57

Bans, weapons and features
  assault weapons, 9, 30–31, 35, 92, 94, 95
  homicide rate effects, 32
  junk guns, 32
  large capacity magazines, 9, 31, 37–38
  National Firearms Act (1934), 7
  public support, 9, 95
  total bans, effects, 41, 42
  See also Gun control laws

Barnes, Collin, 99–100

US-Mexico border violence, 94
US Secret Service, 71
Utah, 63, 68

V

Vehicular homicide, 89–90
Vertigan, Mr., 85
Villahermosa, Jesus, 67, 73
Violence against women. *See* Domestic violence
Violence culture, 34, 42, 79, 82–83
Violence Policy Center, 33
Virginia, gun control laws, 32, 46–47, 59, 69
Virginia Tech shootings (2007), 38, 43, 58–60
    college response, 59–60, 68

first-hand accounts, 43–49
national investigations and response, 59–60, 70–71
police response, 60, 66
weapons source, 46–47, 51, 52

W

Weapons seizures, 93
West Virginia gun laws, 21–22
Western United States, 97, 98, 100
Whitman, Charles, 38
Winters, Ken, 75
Women, violence against. *See* Domestic violence
Workplace protection laws, 62
    See also College campuses
Wright, Stephen E., 36–42